Technology Through Children's Literature

Technology Through Children's Literature

Grades K–5

Holly M. Doe

2003
Teacher Ideas Press
361 Hanover Street
Portsmouth, NH 03802–6926

TEACHER IDEAS PRESS
361 Hanover Street
Portsmouth, NH 03802
www.lu.com/tips

Library of Congress Cataloging-in-Publication Data
ISBN 1–56308–972–6
CIP

Contents

CHAPTER ONE— STORY ELEMENTS

CHAPTER TWO— VOCABULARY

CHAPTER THREE—
GENRE

CHAPTER FOUR—
BOOK REPORTS

CHAPTER FIVE—
MAKING USE OF THE INTERNET

CHAPTER SIX—
AN INTRODUCTION TO ELECTRONIC BOOKS

CHAPTER SEVEN—
COMPREHENSION STRATEGIES

CHAPTER EIGHT—
TECHNOLOGY ACROSS THE CURRICULUM

Acknowledgments

I would like to thank the teachers at North Hampton School for their experience, input, and work that helped to form some of the ideas in this book as well as the wonderful contributions from the students. Special thanks to my mother, a gifted teacher who inspired me to follow in her footsteps and whom I in turn inspired to be an avid user of technology. Finally, thanks to the rest of my family, especially my husband and son, for giving me the time to write.

Introduction

Why use technology with children's literature?

Many schools are adding computers and labs in an effort to teach children how to use "technology." This effort has sometimes been hurried and without thought to why we would want to use technology at all. As a classroom teacher and technology coordinator I have asked myself this question many times. Although I feel it is necessary for my students to have computer skills for the workforce of the twentieth-first century, I also know my job is to teach other concepts and skills. It is therefore essential that when we use technology, we use it to enhance our existing curriculum. If we approach it in this manner then both objectives can be accomplished. Technology needs to be a tool to assist students with their learning and possibly even make a teacher's job easier. If used as a tool, technology can play an integral part in our teaching with children's literature.

This book examines how we use children's literature in our classrooms and explores further possibilities for technology integration. Although this integration requires time, the time is worth the effort. Search for other people in your school who have the expertise to assist you and familiarize yourself with the available software as you might with new math manipulatives. Inevitably, problems emerge with each new project. Improvisation is key to using technology!

As I was writing the activities in this book, I carefully considered the following questions:

- Does technology add a new dimension to learning about literature?

- Does technology motivate students to create a quality project?

- Does technology make my job as a teacher easier?

- Can technology bring more information (not too much information) to my students?

This book supposes that the teacher uses literature every day throughout the curriculum, so it is important to also reflect on how we use literature in the classroom:

- To examine story elements (character, plot, setting, and theme)

- To expose children to a variety of genres

- To learn new vocabulary and other grammar skills

- To provide a model for writing

- To teach a science, math, or social studies concept

- To focus on a specific author

- To respond creatively through book reports and other activities

- To elicit predictions

- To build comprehension strategies

- To connect to our own life experiences

- To read for the pure enjoyment!

These elements of a literature-based reading program will be evident through the activities in each chapter.

How to use this book

This book is written for the classroom teacher as well as technology coordinators, computer teachers, and librarians. This book comprises lesson plans, reproducibles, and samples of student work. The selected literature examples are intended to cover many of the ways we already use literature in our classrooms. Some books provide great examples of character whereas others provide a theme that can be expanded on across the curriculum. It is my hope that each example and corresponding activities should give you ideas to use with many other books. Although each lesson is developed around a favorite classroom picture book or chapter book (even online literature!), the activities are all easily adaptable to a variety of children's books and ages. The chapters range from teaching story elements, comprehension strategies, and genre to the more technology specific topics of the Internet and electronic books. In the last chapter, three books and several activities help to provide a complete picture of how teachers might integrate their entire curriculum around one book title using technology. In the appendices are walk-throughs, additional reproducibles, and resources. Some technology books attempt to teach you how to use the software step by step; this book intends to teach you how to use technology to truly enhance your curriculum. If you've never used some of the software titles, the walk-throughs may assist you. If the walk-throughs are not enough, there is also a list of additional books to provide you with further skills.

The activities in the book are presented in several ways. Some are specifically teacher led, and others involve individual or group work. Many begin with you demonstrating the assignment then allowing students to create their own project. Each activity follows the same format. An example book is chosen to demonstrate each activity followed by the **Overview** that gives a summary of the activity and any useful background knowledge. The **Grade Level** is determined by the activity and not necessarily by the example book. Next is the **Materials** section where any necessary technology hardware and software as well as other supplies are listed. The **Procedure** gives a step-by-step description of the activity including work on and off the computer. The **Extensions and Adaptations** section gives suggestions for modifying the activity or taking it to a higher level. You will often find ways in which to alter the activity for a variety of grade levels. Last, the **Additional Resources** section offers resources such as books, Web sites, and software titles that could help to enhance the activity further.

Suggested Software

The following list of software is used for the lesson plans in this book, but you may substitute other comparable software titles. Keep in mind that the main focus of this book is not the software but the activities and the ways in which technology can be used to enhance teaching and learning.

- *Kid Pix Studio® Deluxe* (Broderbund)–Painting software that has additional features such as Slideshow, Wacky TV, and Stampinator, but its main strengths are the slideshow and painting sections. Any drawing or painting software can be substituted.

- *Inspiration®* (Inspiration Software® Inc.)–Using *Inspiration,* students can create concept-maps, webs, and graphic organizers very quickly. Using an overhead projection device, you can lead the class in a group brainstorm. There are few other software programs that match *Inspiration*'s diagramming capabilities and ease of use.

- *TimeLiner™* 5.0 (Tom Snyder Productions)–This software provides the opportunity for students to create timelines and organize the events in a variety of formats such as a banner. Students can also add graphics and sounds to their timelines and convert them so they can be published on the Web. If you do not have access to *TimeLiner,* students can make a timeline with drawing or painting software.

- *The Amazing Writing Machine®* (The Learning Company)–Students can write and illustrate stories in a storybook format. Students are also able to design simple layouts for text and graphics. There are several similar storybook programs.

- *Hyperstudio®* (Knowledge Adventure®, Inc.)–A multimedia authoring tool that integrates text, sound, graphics, and video. Using its new Internet features, users can create links to Web sites. *Microsoft® Powerpoint,* and *AppleWorks®* slideshow can also be used to create multimedia presentations.

- *AppleWorks®* (Apple® Computer) or *Microsoft® Office* (Microsoft Corporation)–Both software titles include word processing, painting, drawing, spreadsheet, and slideshow capability. *AppleWorks* also includes a database.

Suggested Hardware

Digital Camera–A digital camera is helpful when you want to include a picture in a slideshow, brochure, or other computer-generated project. Photos are saved in a digital format on a disk or other form of media and can be transferred to the computer as soon as the pictures are taken. If you do not have access to a digital camera, you can use a scanner to digitize photos or when you take your regular film in to be processed you can request to have your photos made available on a disk or on the Internet.

Scanner–A scanner can be useful if you have a photo or drawing that is in hard copy format and wish to integrate it into a computer project. The scanner "scans" the photo, digitizes it, and sends it to the computer as a digital image.

Digital Video Camera–A digital video camera is much like a digital camera, but it takes motion video instead. Video is a great motivator for students and allows for creativity. Projects such as interviewing a character or presenting a book review come alive when students have access to video. It is also becoming easier for young students to edit their video and produce a professional-looking product they can be proud of.

Headphones–If you are having students listen to CD-ROM books, create presentations, or play audio files on the computer, you may wish to invest a few dollars in a set of headphones. In a one-computer classroom, the computer is often used throughout the day during busy and quiet times. The computer can become one more distraction that you don't want to fight with. Invest in a pair of headphones, and two students can use the computer at the same time.

Projection Devices–A projection device enables the teacher to demonstrate new software and also allows the students to conduct presentations. Several activities throughout the book begin with you demonstrating or facilitating a discussion using a computer connected to a projection device. Here are the ways in which a computer screen can be projected onto a larger viewing area.

LCD Panel–An LCD panel looks like a thin box with a framed window in the center. It sits on the top of a normal overhead projector and is connected to the computer. The image from the computer is translated to the LCD screen, and when the overhead projector is turned on the light shines through the LCD screen and the image is projected. LCD panels cost approximately $500 to $1000.

Stand-alone Projector–A stand-alone projector needs only to be connected to the computer. Projectors range in quality and can cost anywhere from $2000 to over $10,000.

Scan Converter–A scan converter is a small box that connects a computer to a television. It converts the signal from the computer to a signal that a television can understand. Scan converters cost approximately $100 to $300.

Although it is best to model your lessons using a device as just described, if you do not have access to a projection device you can still always gather your students around a single computer. If you happen to be teaching skills, bring smaller groups up to your computer station for a more individualized lesson and a better view.

Classroom and Lab Management

With each activity, you can choose to have students work independently, in groups, or as a class. These decisions will be based on your obvious resources and the goals of the particular lesson. Here are a few descriptions of a school's possible computer resources and how they can be used.

The Classroom Computer

Many classrooms have one or two computers for many students. Usually this computer is also the station you use for your own record-keeping and e-mail access. In this circumstance, rotating students at the computer one at a time or having small groups complete projects is the best choice. To rotate groups or individuals fairly, create a chart that logs time spent or take a plastic cup and clip clothespins with each student's name to the cup. When students have visited the computer, they can check themselves off the chart or take their clothespin and deposit it inside the cup. When everyone has had some computer time, rotate through again. One computer can also be used to conduct a demonstration or facilitate a discussion.

The Lab

Some schools are fortunate to have a separate computer lab. This is helpful when students need to complete their own assignment with a specific software title, or when you are introducing a new title and want students to gain skills with the software. Labs can also be used for group projects and as a place for your demonstrations. A new trend is to have a mobile lab. With a rolling cart of laptops, different classes can sign the cart out and work in their classroom with more flexibility.

Pods

Pods are groups of three to five computers placed in convenient spots around the classroom. While one student might be word processing a newsletter on one computer, another student could be creating the graphics for the newsletter on another. If you have multiple computer stations or pods, you can have several students or every group working at the same time.

CHAPTER 1

Story Elements

Teaching story elements helps children to recognize the structure of good stories. Story elements also help our students find meaning in the stories they read and give them the skills to become better writers. This chapter specifically explores the story elements of character, setting, and plot. You and your students can better understand these elements and engage in powerful conversations by using concept-mapping software. *Inspiration* software is used in activities throughout this book but most especially in this chapter. Keep in mind that all concept-mapping activities can be done as a class or individually.

Character

Inner Versus Outer Characteristics

Estes, Eleanor. *The Hundred Dresses.* Illustrated by Louis Slobodkin. San Diego: Harcourt Brace, 1974.

OVERVIEW:

Help your students understand the qualities of a character by having the class create a graphic organizer that distinguishes between the character's personality and physical appearance.

GRADE LEVEL:

2–5

MATERIALS:

Inspiration Software

Overhead Projection Device

PROCEDURE:

1. Read aloud *The Hundred Dresses* by Eleanor Estes.

2. After reading, open *Inspiration* and begin by placing the word "Wanda" in the main idea bubble that is in the middle of the screen. To enable class participation, connect your computer to a larger screen with an overhead projection device.

3. Explain to students that they will be examining Wanda's character using *Inspiration*. Ask students to contribute different qualities of Wanda. For example, "Wanda is a good artist."

4. As each characteristic is contributed, add another idea to the screen.

5. When the brainstorming is done, ideas should be scattered all over the screen. Ask students to differentiate between the character's inner and outer characteristics. Sort the ideas into these two categories as the class decides where each characteristic belongs.

6. Create two new ideas for inner and outer characteristics and link the brainstormed characteristics to these categories.

7. Change the idea shapes, fonts, and sizes to make the character map easier to interpret. In the example, you will notice that the girl symbol was chosen to represent Wanda and the "Inner" and "Outer" ideas remained as circles while the characteristics were changed to rectangles (see Figure 1.1). All changes can be made with the Symbol Palette.

8. Discuss as a class which qualities students feel are more important to character development. Why is each characteristic important to the development of a character?

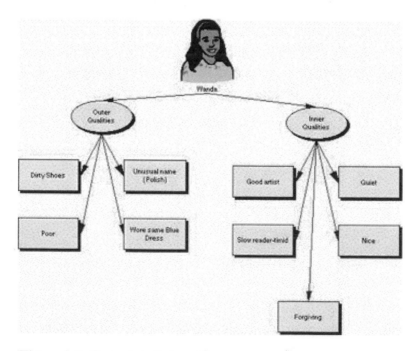

Figure 1.1 Completed character map
This diagram was created using Inspiration® by Inspiration Software®, Inc.

EXTENSIONS AND ADAPTATIONS:

- Have students create similar webs based on characters in a book they are reading or in a story they are writing.

- Sort the characteristics on the screen as students contribute. See if the students can decide how you have grouped the characteristics before you discuss the concept of inner and outer qualities.

- In *Inspiration,* convert the web to an outline format by clicking on the "Outline" button in the upper left-hand corner of the screen (see Figure 1.2). Print the outline and make copies for each student. Have students write a descriptive paragraph about the character using the outline. Demonstrate by writing the first sentence. For example, "Wanda was a poor girl who always wore the same dirty shoes and the same blue dress."

```
Diagram   Add Topic   Add Sub   Add Note   Left
 + Wanda|
  I. + Outer Qualities
    A. - Dirty Shoes
    B. - Unusual name
         (Polish)
    C. - Poor
    D. - Wore same Blue Dress
 II. + Inner Qualities
    A. - Good artist
    B. - Quiet
    C. - Slow reader-timid
    D. - Nice
    E. - Forgiving
```

Figure 1.2 Character map displayed in outline format
This diagram was created using Inspiration® by Inspiration Software®, Inc.

ADDITIONAL RESOURCE:

Inspiration Walk-through in Appendix A

Character Detectives

Gantos, Jack. *Joey Pigza Swallowed the Key.* New York: Farrar, Straus and Giroux, 1998.

OVERVIEW:

Characters can be revealed through their actions, thoughts, conversations, and feelings toward other characters. Use a graphic organizer to brainstorm qualities and turn your students into character detectives.

GRADE LEVEL:

3–5

MATERIALS:

Inspiration Software

Overhead Projection Device

PROCEDURE:

1. After reading *Joey Pigza Swallowed the Key,* discuss as a class the character of Joey.

2. As a class, brainstorm the qualities of Joey using *Inspiration* software and an overhead projection device. These characteristics can be both inner and outer like the previous activity. Joey's name should be in the main idea bubble in the center of the screen, and the characteristics should be linked around the Joey bubble.

3. When the class has generated several qualities, select one and discuss as a class how students knew that about the character of Joey. Was it through an action by the character or was it through something the character or another person in the book said? If not, was it something the author indicated through narration?

4. Click on the arrow that connects the characteristic to the character's name and record how the quality was determined (action, conversation, narration, or comment of others) (see Figure 1.3). Record the evidence with a quote from the book or a description of the action. Students use their books to act as detectives in finding the proof.

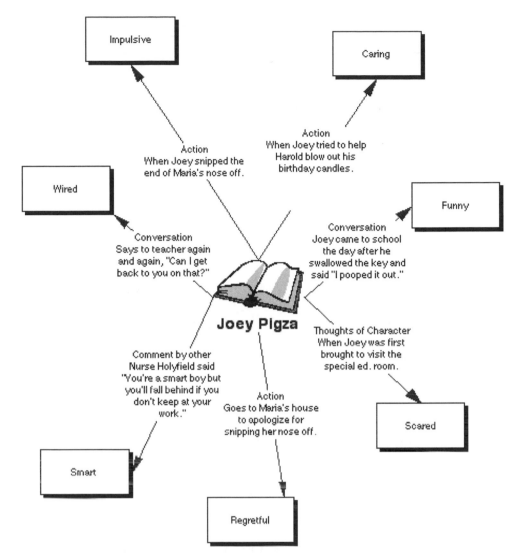

Figure 1.3 Graphic organizer of Joey's qualities with evidence

This diagram was created using Inspiration® by Inspiration Software®, Inc.

EXTENSIONS AND ADAPTATIONS:

- View the diagram in outline format. Instead of recording just one example of how Joey was "wired," have students record two or three instances below each quality.

- Instead of using a graphic organizer, use a spreadsheet application like *Apple-Works* to record the same information. Insert a header for the character's name and fill in the top row as shown in the example. The specific qualities can then be listed down the first column and the evidence can be listed under the way in which it was discovered (see Figure 1.4).

Joey Pigza

	A	B	C	D	E
1	Qualities	Actions	Conversation	Narration	others
2					
3					

Figure 1.4 Spreadsheet template for recording qualities of Joey with evidence

ADDITIONAL RESOURCE:

Inspiration Walk-through in Appendix A

Character Letterhead

Cooney, Barbara. *Miss Rumphius.* New York: Viking Penguin Inc., 1982.

OVERVIEW:

Although this activity focuses on character qualities, it also requires students to use their word processing skills. After examining a character in their book, students create a letterhead file on the computer that relays the qualities of the character.

GRADE LEVEL:

2–5

MATERIALS:

Word Processing Software *(AppleWorks* or *Microsoft Word)*

Examples of letterheads

PROCEDURE:

1. Introduce the concept of a letterhead by showing examples to students of a variety of individual and business letterheads. Discuss what the styles of the letterheads lead us to believe about the person or business. (I always like to include my own personal example.)

2. Ask students to think about the characters in the book they have completed reading. In this example, the character is Miss Rumphius. What would her letterhead look like? Consider font, size, style, color, and graphics.

3. Have students create a draft on paper before they move to the computer.

4. Using the computer, have students create the final draft of their character's letterhead. In most word processing software there is a clip-art library or students can use an online gallery of clip-art (see Figure 1.5).

5. When completed, ask students to open a word processing file and type a paragraph explaining their choices in relation to their character's likes, dislikes, and overall personality.

The following description accompanied Miss Rumphius's letterhead.

Miss Rumphius wanted to travel the world and live by the sea. Her grandfather told her she must also make the world more beautiful. She did this by planting lupines all over her town by the sea so I put lupines at the top of the letterhead. In the book she reminded her nieces and nephews to make the world more beautiful so I put those words at the bottom of the page. I picked the font because it looks pretty like books in a library, and her address is supposed to be an ocean address so I picked Maine.

Figure 1.5 Final draft of Miss Rumphius's letterhead

EXTENSIONS AND ADAPTATIONS:

- Use the letterhead by having students write a letter to another character in the book from the main character's perspective. Students can handwrite or type the letter on the computer.

- Have students develop their own personal letterhead file.

- Create an entire office set for your character (business cards, envelopes, etc.).

ADDITIONAL RESOURCES:

Ahlberg, Janet and Allan. *The Jolly Postman or other People's Letters.* Boston: Little, Brown and Company, 1986. This book has great examples of envelopes and letterhead from fairy tale characters.

The Jolly Postman's Party CD. Published by Dorling Kindersley Publishing, Inc. Students can create postcards, letters, and other items with this software package.

Google Image Surfer: **http://images.google.com.** This section of the Google Search site allows the user to search specifically for images. Type in a search word, and you will be presented with thumbnail images from a variety of Web sites.

Character Analysis with a Spreadsheet

Fendler, Donn. *Lost on a Mountain in Maine.* Edited by Joseph B. Egan. New York: Beech Tree Books, 1992.

OVERVIEW:

Characters are sometimes referred to as "round," meaning that they are dynamic and change throughout the course of the book. A histogram provides a way to chart the changes of a rounded character throughout a story. Using a spreadsheet, students can create a histogram and see how the character reacted to different events throughout the story.

GRADE LEVEL:

3–5

MATERIALS:

Spreadsheet Software *(AppleWorks* or *Microsoft® Excel)*

Overhead Projection Device (Optional)

PROCEDURE:

1. Have your class read a book like *Lost on a Mountain in Maine* by Donn Fendler. (In Maine, many fourth grades read this when they are in the midst of their Maine state studies. It is also a terrific book if your students enjoy the survival theme.)

2. Generate character qualities as a class or have students revisit their reading journals to find words they may have used to describe Donn. You could also handpick the qualities for a speedier process.

3. To prepare for the histogram, set up a spreadsheet like the next example (see Figure 1.6). List the qualities of the character down the first column. Across the top row, enter "Beginning of Story," "Middle of Story," and "End of Story." (You could also break the rows into chapter titles such as Chapters 1–4, Chapters 5–9, and Chapters 10–15.)

Title of Book: Lost on a Mountain in Maine
Author: Donn Fendler as told to Joseph B. Egan
Name of Character: Donn Fendler

	A	B	C	D
1		Beginning of Story	Middle of Story	End of Story
2	Courageous	9	9	9
3	Hopeful	7	8	4
4	Fearful	4	5	6
5	Sanity	0	8	7
6	Survival Instincts	5	5	7
7	Faith	6	8	9
8	Physical Strength	10	5	2

Figure 1.6 Completed analysis of Donn Fendler using a spreadsheet

4. Insert a header into the spreadsheet and type, "Title of Book," "Author," and "Name of Character."

5. Save the file as a template so it can be used again by students.

6. Have students as a class or independently open the template on the computer and fill in numbers in each column to rate the degree to which the character exhibits each quality listed. For example, when examining Donn's courage, a "1" would indicate that his courage was very low whereas a "10" would signify strong courage.

7. When the spreadsheet is filled in, highlight all the information entered into the spreadsheet and select the "Make a Chart" command in *Appleworks* or the "Chart" command in *Microsoft Excel*. Select a line chart from the choices and make other changes to the graph such as adding a title (see Figure 1.7).

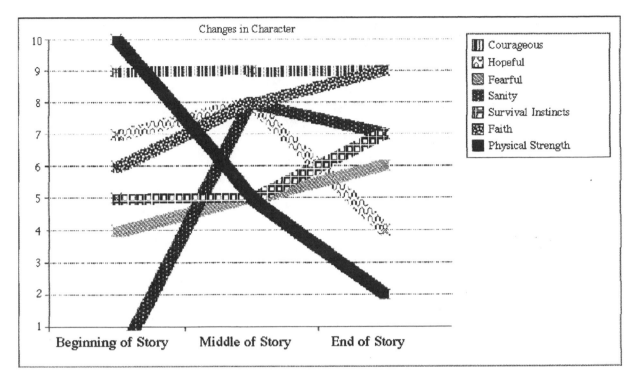

Figure 1.7 Line chart displaying changes in Donn Fendler's qualities

EXTENSIONS AND ADAPTATIONS:

- Break the class into groups and have each group complete a histogram on the same character. Compare the completed charts. Have students back up their choices with evidence from the book.

- Create a histogram that focuses on one specific quality of a character. List important events down the first column and rate the degree to which the character exhibits the specific quality in the second column (see Figure 1.8).

Title of Book:
Author:
Name of character:
Quality:

	A	B
1	Event 1	8
2	Event 2	4
3	Event 3	10
4	Event 4	9
5	Event 5	10

Figure 1.8 Example of histogram with focus on one character quality

- Next, make a line chart (see Figure 1.9) and analyze what happened to the character throughout the story.

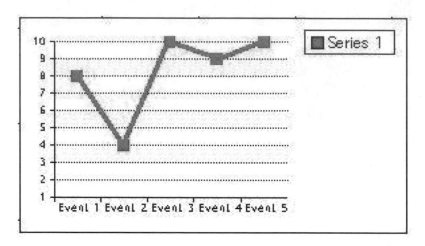

Figure 1.9 Example of line chart displaying changes in one character quality

ADDITIONAL RESOURCES:

Spreadsheet Walk-through in Appendix A

Saving Templates Walk-through in Appendix A

Character Timeline

Wilder, Laura Ingalls. *Little House on the Prairie.* New York: HarperCollins, 1953.

OVERVIEW:

Use a timeline to examine the course of events from a character's perspective. With a program like *TimeLiner,* a timeline can be created quickly and customized to show negative and positive life events.

GRADE LEVEL:

3–5

MATERIALS:

TimeLiner Software

PROCEDURE:

1. Have students read a chapter book such as *Little House on the Prairie* by Laura Ingalls Wilder. While reading the book, have students keep track of major events in the character's life in reading journals.

2. To begin a timeline, have your students open the program *TimeLiner* and choose **Custom Timeline.** At the next prompt enter the word "Event" and click in the bullet that says "Put label before value" (see Figure 1.10).

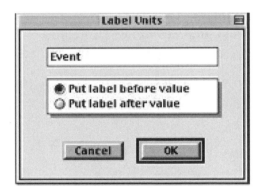

Figure 1.10 First window prompt after choosing Custom Timeline

3. Students should list all the main events in the character's life in the "What" column. In the "When" column type 1, 2, 3, etc. The word "Event" should automatically precede each number (see Figure 1.11).

When	What
Event 1	Laura leaves the woods of Wisconsin to go west with her family.
Event 2	Laura loses her dog Jack in the creek.
Event 3	Jack finds his way back to Laura and her family.
Event 4	Pa picks a spot for their new home and builds a log cabin.
Event 5	Laura meets the Indians for the first time.
Event 6	Laura takes her first cold drink from the well.
Event 7	Laura, Pa, and Mary visit the Indian camp and find beautiful beads.
Event 8	Laura and her family become sick with Malaria.
Event 9	Mr. Edwards brings presents from Santa to Laura and Mary.
Event 10	Pa goes to town and brings back pretty combs for Laura and Mary.
Event 11	A prairie fire comes close to the house but doesn't burn it.
Event 12	The Indians leave to go further west.
Event 13	Laura and Mary help to plant their first garden.
Event 14	Laura and her family have to leave their home.

Figure 1.11 View of data format

4. When students have entered all the character's life events, they can convert the data into banner format by clicking on the button with flags (see Figure 1.12).

Figure 1.12 Buttons to choose various formats in *Timeliner*

5. Have students format their banner by changing the flags and adding a title. To move a flag, drag the flag up or down. To change a flag's shape, click on the right end of the flag and drag to the desired shape. To add a title, locate the command "New title ..." under the Edit menu. Also, show the difference between negative and positive events in a character's life by changing the styles or fonts of the flags using the format menu. Encourage students to add graphics to their timelines (see Figure 1.13). The graphic in the example was created in *Kid Pix,* copied, and pasted into *TimeLiner.*

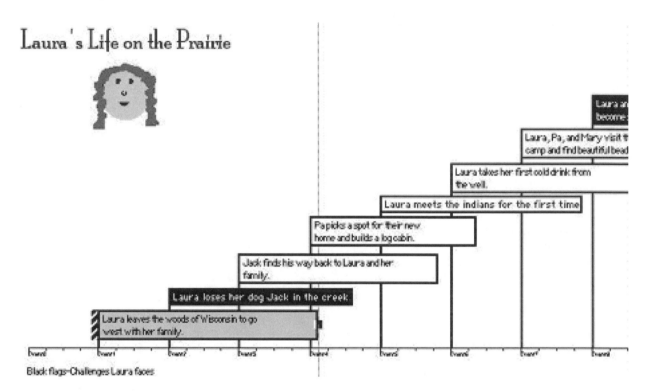

Figure 1.13 Completed timeline of Laura Ingalls Wilder's life events
This timeline was created using TimeLiner ™ 5.0 by Tom Snyder Productions.

EXTENSIONS AND ADAPTATIONS:

- Create timelines for each character in the story. Be sure to include only the events that affect the specific character. Compare and contrast the completed timelines.

- This activity can also be used to examine the sequence of events or the conflicts and solutions of the overall plot as they unfold instead of focusing on the element of character.

- If you do not own *TimeLiner* software, use a drawing program to create a character timeline.

ADDITIONAL RESOURCES:

Copy/Paste and Online Clip-art Walk-through in Appendix A

Google Image Surfer: **http://images.google.com**. This section of the Google Search site allows the user to search specifically for images. Type in a search word, and you will be presented with thumbnail images from a variety of Web sites.

Plot

Problems and Solutions

White, E. B. *Stuart Little.* Illustrated by Garth Williams. New York: HarperCollins, 1945.

OVERVIEW:

Examine the plot of a story by identifying the problems the character faces and how the character attempts to solve them. To help students better understand the plot of the story, have them create a graphic organizer of the problems and solutions in the book.

GRADE LEVEL:

3–5

MATERIALS:

Inspiration Software

Overhead Projection Device (Optional)

PROCEDURE:

1. As students read their book, have them keep track of the problems that the main character faces and the attempts at solving each problem. Students can record problems and solutions in a reading journal.

2. If the entire class is reading the book, have students share and discuss the lists they have generated.

3. With *Inspiration,* begin two graphic organizers side by side. One will link the problems, and the other will link the solutions.

4. Using the Symbol Palette on the left-hand side of the screen, have students use co-ordinating symbols for the corresponding problems and solutions. In the example, the teacher used the Number Palette to pair the problems with the solutions. Problem 1 matches to Solution 1, etc. (see Figure 1.14).

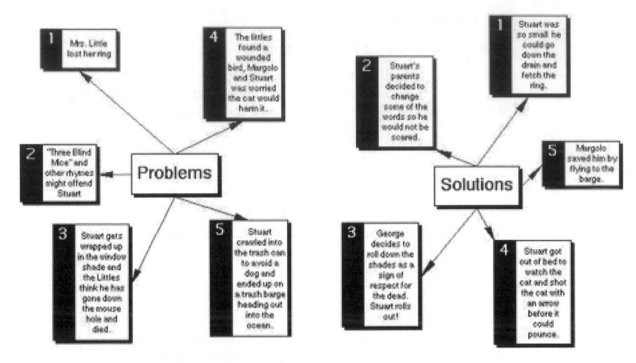

Figure 1.14 Completed problem and solution graphic organizer
This diagram was created using Inspiration® by Inspiration Software®, Inc.

EXTENSIONS AND ADAPTATIONS:

- Create a third graphic organizer listing other possible solutions that the author could have considered.

- Choose one problem in the story and brainstorm all the possible solutions including the solution reached in the story.

- Highlight the major problem in the story by choosing a special symbol such as a star.

ADDITIONAL RESOURCE:

Inspiration Walk-through in Appendix A

Events Flow Chart

Lionni, Leo. *Swimmy.* New York: Pantheon Books, 1968.

OVERVIEW:

Students can recall the events of a story and determine how each event led to the next using the words *and, but, then,* and *so.*

GRADE LEVEL:

    1–4

MATERIALS:

    Inspiration Software

    Overhead Projection Device

PROCEDURE:

1. After reading the book aloud, begin a class brainstorm in *Inspiration* recalling the major events in a story. Have a copy of the book in case an event is forgotten or the order of events is in dispute. Use an overhead projection device to display the screen for all students to see.

2. When completed, link each event in order and in a clockwise circular pattern. Connect each item to the next with an arrow.

3. On each arrow decide which word (and, but, so, then) fits the circumstances of the plot. Click in the middle of each line to type the word that applies (see Figure 1.15).

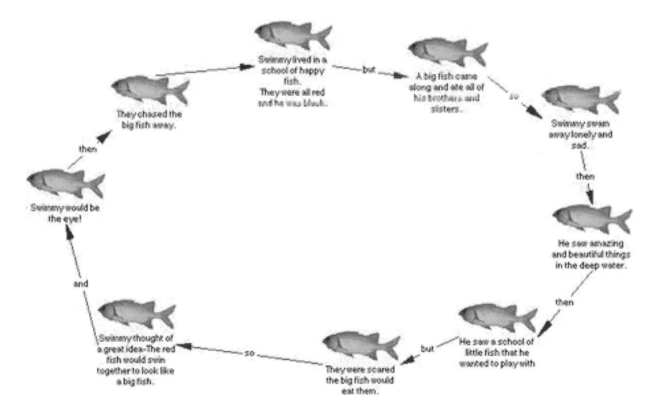

Figure 1.15 Completed events flow chart

This diagram was created using Inspiration® by Inspiration Software®, Inc.

EXTENSIONS AND ADAPTATIONS:

For younger students, create a simpler chart using the words "wanted," "but," and "so" (see Figure 1.16). Use this simple flow chart to create a one-paragraph summary of the problem and solution in the story.

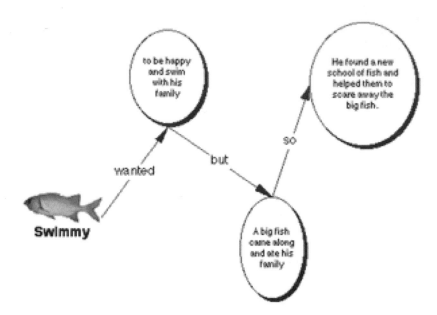

Figure 1.16 Example of simpler events flow chart
This diagram was created using Inspiration® by Inspiration Software®, Inc.

ADDITIONAL RESOURCES:

Inspiration Walk-through in Appendix A

Books:

Aardema, Verna. *Why Mosquitoes Buzz in People's Ears.* New York: The Dial Press, 1975.
Numeroff, Laura Joffe. *If You Give a Mouse a Cookie.* Illustrated by Felicia Bond. New York: Harper, 1985.

The Mixed-Up Slideshow

Carle, Eric. *Pancakes, Pancakes!* New York: Simon and Schuster, 1990.

OVERVIEW:

In this activity, students use the computer to create pictures of the major events throughout a story. After you mix up the pictures in a computer slideshow, students attempt to put them back into the right order. This activity helps students to build sequencing skills and recall the main events in the story.

GRADE LEVEL:

K–3

MATERIALS:

Painting and Slideshow Software (*Kid Pix Studio Deluxe*)

Inspiration Software

PROCEDURE:

1. Read aloud *Pancakes, Pancakes!* to your class.

2. Using *Inspiration,* brainstorm with your class what Jack needed to make a pancake. Use an overhead projection device connected to your computer so the whole class can participate.

3. After brainstorming the events, arrange them into a flow chart (see Figure 1.17).

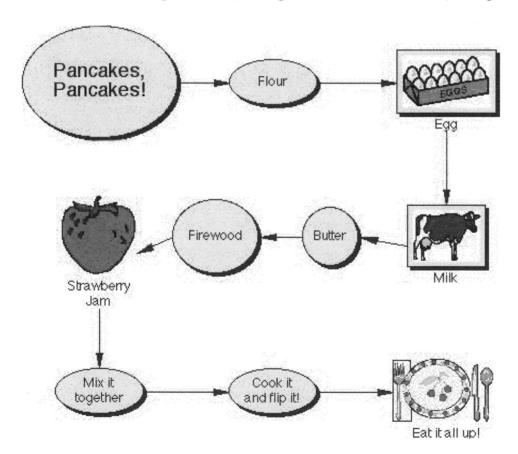

Figure 1.17 Flow chart of events from *Pancakes, Pancakes!*
This diagram was created using Inspiration® by Inspiration Software®, Inc.

4. Have each student or small groups of students be responsible for illustrating an event from the book using a program like *Kid Pix* (see Figure 1.18).

Figure 1.18 Illustration of one event in *Pancakes, Pancakes!*
Taken from Kid Pix® Studio. ©Broderbund Properties LLC. Used with permission.

5. When all the pictures are finished, collect the pictures and assemble them into a slideshow (see Figure 1.19). Mix up the order of the slides by clicking on the trucks and dragging them to new positions.

6. Have students take turns visiting the computer and trying to put the slides in the correct order. In *Kid Pix,* students can double-click on a picture and see a larger version of it. To move slides, drag a truck to a new position. At any point students can hit the "Play" button to get feedback on how they are doing. (Be sure to save the mixed-up copy of the slideshow so each student can start with the original mixed-up version.)

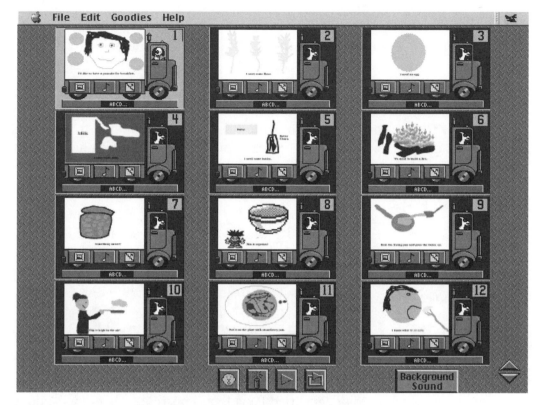

Figure 1.19 Completed slideshow from *Pancakes, Pancakes!*
Taken from Kid Pix® Studio. ©Broderbund Properties LLC. Used with permission.

EXTENSIONS AND ADAPTATIONS:

- If your school has a scanner, students can draw their pictures with crayons or markers and scan them for the slideshow.

- For chapter books, have one student be responsible for drawing a main event from each chapter.

ADDITIONAL RESOURCES:

Kid Pix Walk-through in Appendix A

Kid Pix Planning Sheet in Appendix B

The Official Eric Carle Website: **http://www.eric-carle.com**. This author site contains information on new and old books, events, artwork, and a section for Frequently Asked Questions.

Finish a Fairy Tale

Brett, Jan. *Goldilocks and the Three Bears.* New York: G. P. Putnam and Sons, 1990.

OVERVIEW:

This activity allows students to demonstrate that they comprehend the reading through their illustrations while also using their sequencing skills to finish the story. Students are given a template with a portion of a fairy tale written and space to illustrate the story and give it an ending.

GRADE LEVEL:

K–3

MATERIALS:

Storybook Software (*The Amazing Writing Machine*)

PROCEDURE:

1. Read a favorite fairy tale like *Goldilocks and the Three Bears* to your students. While reading the story, ask the students to predict what is going to happen next. For example, after Goldilocks tried Papa Bear's porridge what did she do next?

2. Using a storybook program like *The Amazing Writing Machine,* create a template by typing in the text of the fairy tale (see Figures 1.20 and 1.21). Leave spaces for illustrations above the text or on the following page. To shorten the length, you may want to summarize the plot. Complete half of the story so that the students can write in the ending. In *Goldilocks and the Three Bears,* stop typing the story after Goldilocks tries the three different size chairs.

3. Using the template, ask students to illustrate each page of the story. When they come to the page where the story ends, ask them to complete and illustrate it on their own.

Figure 1.20 Template cover

Figure 1.21 Template page with space for students to illustrate the story

EXTENSIONS AND ADAPTATIONS:

- For students who struggle with drawing on the computer or have difficulty with fine motor skills, look for clip-art and find items that would be helpful with the chosen story. (In *The Amazing Writing Machine,* there is a "Stamp" tool with a great variety of images including the three bears!)

- See if your program has the capability to read the text aloud for emergent or nonreaders. (In *The Amazing Writing Machine,* highlight the words and click on the "Robot" tool to have your text read aloud.)

- This activity requires a lot of help for younger students. Enlist volunteers to assist students with the writing portion of the project or read aloud the story to beginning readers. You could also write the entire story so students only need to complete the illustrations.

ADDITIONAL RESOURCES:

Jan Brett's Homepage: **http://www.janbrett.com**. This author site contains downloadable coloring pages, artwork contests, new book information, online video chats, and several other book-related activities.

Other versions of the Three Bears:

Marshall, James. *Goldilocks and the Three Bears.* New York: Dial Books for Young Readers, 1988.

Gorbachev, Valeri. *Goldilocks and the Three Bears.* New York: North-South Books, 2001.

Online Fairy Tales:

Aesop's Fables—Online Collection: **http://www.aesopfables.com**
The SurLaLune Fairy Tale Site: **http://members.aol.com/surlalune/frytales**

These two sites contain text files for a variety of fairy tales and Aesop's fables. Use them to copy and paste text into another program.

Setting

Make a Book Map

Lewis, C. S. *The Lion, the Witch and the Wardrobe.* Illustrated by Pauline Baynes. New York: HarperCollins, 1994.

OVERVIEW:

Some authors include maps of their story settings to help the readers identify with the events and setting of a story. Using a drawing program, students will create a birds-eye view of the setting(s) in their story.

GRADE LEVEL:

3–5

MATERIALS:

Painting or drawing software *(Kid Pix Studio Deluxe)*

Clip-art collection of maps and symbols (optional)

Example of books that use maps

PROCEDURE:

1. Show students examples of books where the author included a map to help the reader recognize the setting of the story. Discuss how a map can assist the reader.

2. After reading the book, have students list all the major settings or locations of *The Lion, the Witch and the Wardrobe* in a reading journal. Look for clues in the reading that help to determine one location's proximity and direction to another location.

3. Prepare a preliminary sketch of the map from a birds-eye view and determine whether clip-art will be needed before you begin.

4. Draw the map in a drawing program like *Kid Pix*. Create a key with appropriate symbols and add a title to the map (see Figure 1.22).

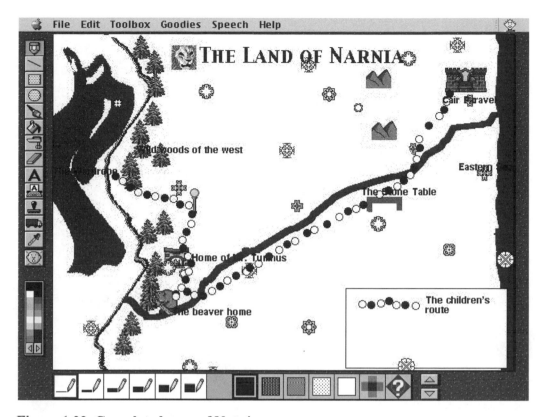

Figure 1.22 Completed map of Narnia

Taken from Kid Pix® Studio. ©Broderbund Properties LLC. Used with permission.

EXTENSIONS AND ADAPTATIONS:

Although this activity allows students to think creatively about the settings in a book, it can also be used to help students with their geography skills. Here are some titles in which students can use a world or U.S. map to find the specific locations mentioned in the story.

Priceman, Marjorie. *How to Make an Apple Pie and See the World.* New York: Alfred A. Knopf, 1994.

Knight, Margy Burns. *Talking Walls.* Illustrated by Anne Sibley O'Brien. Gardiner, Maine: Tilbury House Publishers, 1992.

ADDITIONAL RESOURCES:

Kid Pix Walkthrough in Appendix A

Kid Pix Planning Sheet in Appendix B

Web sites:

Narnia.com: **http://www.narnia.com**. This site contains a map of Narnia and other information on the Chronicles of Narnia. Use the map as a comparison after students complete their own maps.

MapQuest: **http://www.mapquest.com**. MapQuest allows the user to create maps of existing locations around the world.

Software:

Mapmakers Toolkit® by Tom Snyder Productions. This software allows students to make maps of states, countries, and continents. Students can add their own text and stamps to label the maps. (Grades 3–5)

Neighborhood Map Machine® by Tom Snyder Productions. This software allows students to create simpler maps with streets, houses, and trees.

Other books with maps:

Jacques, Brian. *Redwall.* New York: Philomel Books, 1986.
Gurney, James. *Dinotopia.* Atlanta: Turner Publishing, Inc., 1992.
Juster, Norton. *The Phantom Tollbooth.* New York: Random House, Inc., 1961.

Timeline of Settings

Gurney, James. *Dinotopia.* Atlanta: Turner Publishing, Inc., 1992.

OVERVIEW:

Timelines can help students to recall the major events or settings in a story. In this activity, the book *Dinotopia* is used to create a timeline of the beautifully described settings that the characters visit.

GRADE LEVEL:

2–5

MATERIALS:

TimeLiner Software

PROCEDURE:

1. Have students read a book like *Dinotopia* by James Gurney. While reading the book, students can keep track of settings in a reading journal.

2. To begin a timeline, have your students open the program *TimeLiner* and choose **Custom Timeline.** At the next prompt, enter the word "Location" and click in the bullet that says "Put label before value" (see Figure 1.23).

Figure 1.23 First window prompt after choosing Custom Timeline

3. Students should list all the settings of the book in the "What" column. In the "When" column, type 1, 2, 3, etc. The word "Location" should automatically precede each number (see Figure 1.24).

	When	What
	Location1	Arthur and Will Denison departed from Boston.
	Location2	Deserted on a beach with dinosaurs!
	Location3	Girl leads them to the Egg Hatchery
	Location4	They go to the city of Pooktook
	Location5	A settlement near Volcaneum

Figure 1.24 View of data format

4. After students have entered all the story's settings, they can convert the data into a banner format by clicking on the button with flags (see Figure 1.25).

Figure 1.25 Buttons to choose various formats in *Timeliner*

5. Have students format their banner by changing the flags and adding a title. To move a flag, drag the flag up or down. To change a flag's shape, click on the right end of the flag and drag to the desired shape. To add a title, look for "New title ..." under the Edit menu. They can also change the styles or fonts of the flags using the format menu. Encourage students to add graphics to their timelines (see Figure 1.26).

6. While looking at the finished timelines, discuss which settings were students' favorites. Which one would they most like to visit?

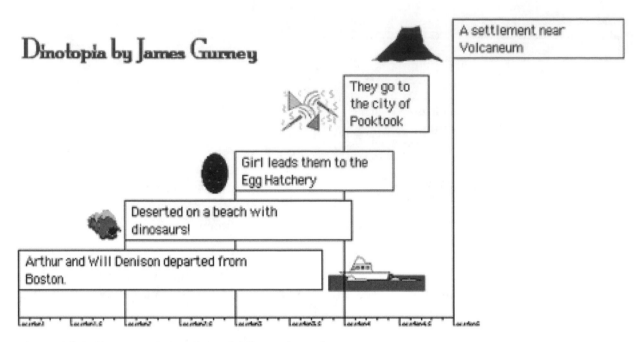

Figure 1.26 Completed timeline of *Dinotopia* settings

This timeline was created using TimeLiner™ 5.0 by Tom Snyder Productions.

EXTENSIONS AND ADAPTATIONS:

- Invent a new setting in *Dinotopia* for the father to explore. Use a drawing program to portray the new setting.

- If you do not own *TimeLiner* software, use a drawing program to create a timeline of settings.

ADDITIONAL RESOURCE:

Dinotopia: The Official Website: **http://www.dinotopia.com**

Compare and Contrast of Settings

Say, Allen. *Grandfather's Journey.* Boston: Houghton Mifflin Company, 1993.

OVERVIEW:

Using *Inspiration,* students use their critical thinking skills to compare and contrast the two different settings of California and Japan.

GRADE LEVEL:

3–5

MATERIALS:

Inspiration Software

Overhead Projection Device

PROCEDURE:

1. In *Inspiration,* create two or more idea bubbles listing the settings in the book. Leave space between the ideas to generate words for similarities of the settings and leave the outside space for differences (similar to a Venn diagram).

2. Choose a book like *Grandfather's Journey* by Allen Say that has two distinctive settings. After reading the book, have students discuss the differences and similarities between the two settings. (I encourage students to use prior knowledge as well as the facts they have gathered from the story.) Using an overhead projection device connected to your computer, add to the *Inspiration* template as students generate similarities and differences.

3. Connect the differences and similarities to the two setting ideas with arrows.

4. Last, using the "A" tool found at the bottom of the screen, create text boxes to add the words "Differences" and "Similarities" above the ideas they represent. Create another text box and add the title and author at the top of the diagram (see Figure 1.27).

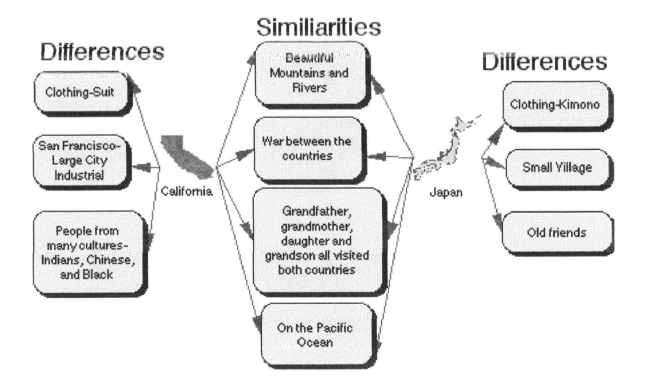

Figure 1.27 Completed diagram of comparisons between California and Japan

This diagram was created using Inspiration® by Inspiration Software®, Inc.

EXTENSIONS AND ADAPTATIONS:

- Create one side of "Differences" and see if students can identify an opposing difference for the opposite side.

- Compare and contrast the main settings from two different books.

ADDITIONAL RESOURCE:

Inspiration Walk-through in Appendix A

All of the Elements

Story Elements Brochure

Clements, Andrew. *Frindle.* Illustrated by Brian Selznick. New York: Simon and Schuster, 1996.

OVERVIEW:

A brochure describing the elements of a story helps to reinforce summary skills. Students create a brochure that describes the elements and allows space for a small review.

GRADE LEVEL:

3–5

MATERIALS:

Word Processing Software *(AppleWorks* or *Microsoft Word)*

Brochure Planning Sheet Reproducible

PROCEDURE:

1. Have students complete the planning sheet before they begin their work on the computer. This ensures that time on the computer is spent wisely.

2. Locate a template of a brochure in either *AppleWorks* or *Microsoft Word.* If you wish, alter the template to appear similar to the planning sheet or design your own template.

3. After reading *Frindle* as a class or individually, have students open the teacher-created template. Give a quick lesson using the computer and an overhead projection device to show how to alter the template so students can add their own graphics and text. Explain that the first page of the template is the cover, inside flap, and back. The second page is what you see when the brochure is completely open. If possible, have examples of brochures from bookstores, libraries, or local businesses.

4. On the front cover, students should type the title, author, and any other important information. A graphic should also be added. The back of the brochure should contain a quick review of the book, and the inside flap should list the genre, appropriate age or audience, and an About the Author section (see Figure 1.28).

5. On the inside or second page of the template is the space to describe the characters, plot, and setting. If students need guidelines for the brochure, copy the example from *Frindle* (see Figure 1.29).

6. When the brochures are completed and spell-checked, print them out and fold them together. Have students share their brochures with each other or post the brochures to intrigue students who are looking for a new book to read (see Figures 1.30 and 1.31).

EXTENSIONS AND ADAPTATIONS:

- Have students use the brochure format to generate the details for their own story.

- Create a brochure that focuses on only one story element such as character.

ADDITIONAL RESOURCE:

Saving templates Walk-through in Appendix A

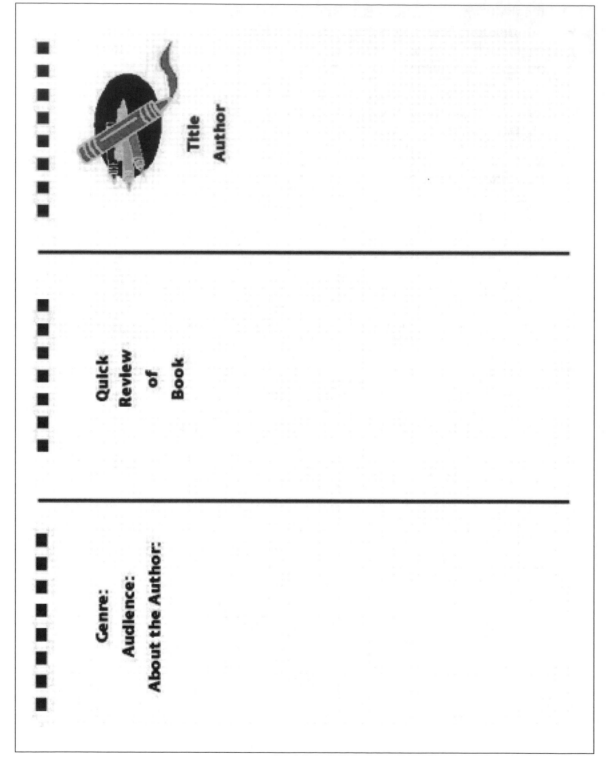

Figure 1.28 Template for cover, inside flap, and back of brochure

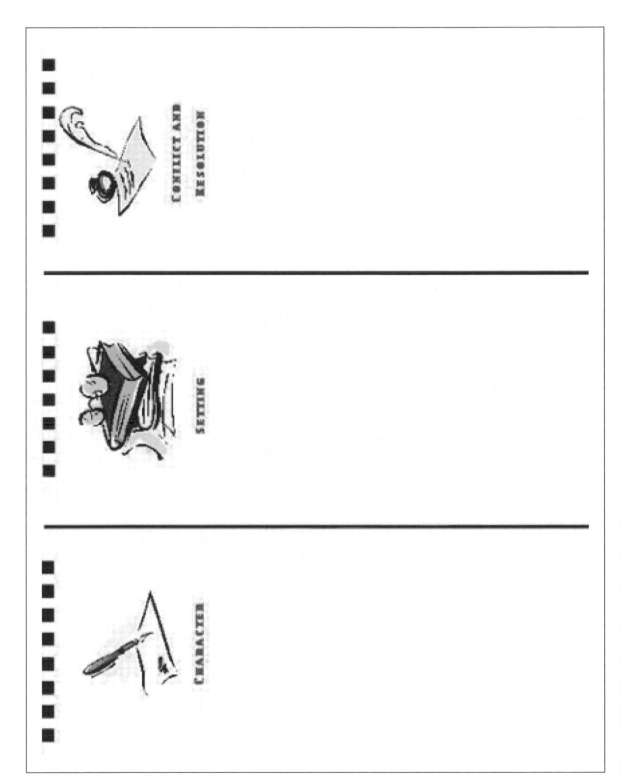

Figure 1.29 Template for inside of brochure

FRINDLE
BY ANDREW CLEMENTS

Book Review

Frindle is a very funny book about a creative kid named Nick and his teacher, Ms. Granger. It is amazing what happens to Nick when he invents a different word for pen. Before he knows it, everyone is calling a pen a "frindle." This book makes me want to invent a crazy word. It also makes you think alot about where words came from.

I would recommend this book to any fourth or fifth grader who needs a good laugh.

Genre: Realistic Fiction

Audience: 3-5

About the Author:

Andrew Clements lives in Westborough, Massachusetts. He is also the author of *Big A!* and *Billy and the Bad Teacher*. He was a teacher for seven years near Chicago. Then he moved to New England for a career in publishing.

Figure 1.30 Completed cover, inside flap, and back of brochure

CHARACTERS

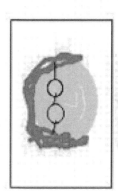

Nick Allen is a fifth grader with red hair and glasses. He is liked by most kids.

Nick is creative and smart. He is not a bad kid, but I would not call him an angel either. He is known for stalling his teachers so sometimes the class does not have time to get a homework assignment.

Nick got alot of attention from newspapers and television for his new word. In one part, his teacher notices that he has become alot quieter and withdrawn. He still had alot of great ideas, but he didn't dare share them because he thought he would get in trouble. Ms. Granger reminds him to be himself.

SETTING

Welcome to
Westfield
Home of the original
frindle!

This story takes place in Westfield, New Hampshire. Westfield is a small town that is usually quite quiet. Nick Allen makes Westfield famous with his new word, Frindle!

Alot of the story also takes place in Lincoln Elementary school during their fifth grade year.

PLOT

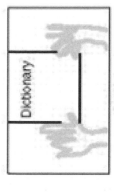

Dictionary

Nick asks his teacher, Ms. Granger, "who says that dog means dog." Ms. Granger said that Nick and other people say that dog means dog. So Nick and his friends make an oath to call a pen a frindle. This makes Ms. Granger annoyed and she tries to make the kids stop saying the new word. They don't stop though. They would rather serve detention than stop saying frindle. Soon frindle spreads all over town and around the world. Nick can't control his word. It belongs to everyone.

In the end we find out that Ms. Granger helped Nick's word out by acting like she thought it was a stupid idea. Nick's word gets in the dictionary.

Figure 1.31 Completed inside of brochure

Visualizing the Elements

De Beer, Hans. *Little Polar Bear*. New York: Scholastic Inc., 1995.

OVERVIEW:

Inspiration can be used to analyze the individual elements of stories as well as looking at the whole picture. This activity uses a teacher-created template to help students understand all the elements of a good story.

GRADE LEVEL:

1–5

MATERIALS:

Inspiration Software

Overhead Projection Device

PROCEDURE:

1. Create a template for the elements of a story. The main idea bubble should contain the name of the book, and the outside ideas should be labeled for the elements of the story (character, setting, plot, etc.). In the case of plot, create two more connecting ideas for the problem and solution (see Figure 1.32).

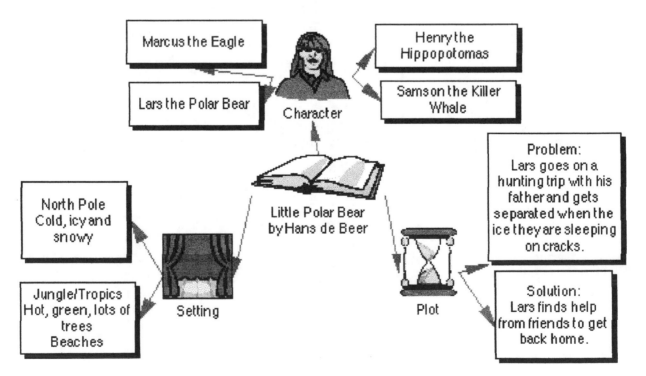

Figure 1.32 Completed story elements diagram

This diagram was created using Inspiration® by Inspiration Software®, Inc.

2. Read a story to your students that clearly demonstrates the elements such as *Little Polar Bear* by Hans de Beer.

3. As a class, fill in the template using a computer connected to an overhead projection device. When possible, use additional ideas to generate more information about a character for example. There also may be more than one setting.

EXTENSIONS AND ADAPTATIONS:

- Print an empty template to assist students in generating the details for their own stories.

- Do this activity throughout the school year with each read-aloud. Keep printed copies of each diagram in a three-ring binder and compare each story's development. Do the better stories have something in common? Do students like stories with several plots or just one? (This will probably depend on the age and comprehension level of your students.)

- Add other elements to the diagram such as theme and genre.

ADDITIONAL RESOURCE:

Inspiration Walk-through in Appendix A

CHAPTER 2

Vocabulary

When we typically think of vocabulary activities, we think of basal-type texts with simple, planned words. Likewise, when we think of technology and vocabulary we think of skill and drill software that has no connection to real literature. Although there are several individualized skill and drill software programs that do help children acquire new vocabulary, there are also many ways for children to organize and acquire definitions using productivity software (i.e., database, word processing, and drawing) with connections to word-rich literature.

Word Web

Lowry, Lois. *Number the Stars.* New York: Bantam Doubleday Dell Publishing Group, Inc., 1989.

OVERVIEW:

Students will web a single word in *Inspiration.* Looking at one word in-depth allows students to examine not only the definitions but also synonyms, antonyms, and how the word was used in the context of the reading.

GRADE LEVEL:

3–5

MATERIALS:

Inspiration Software

Overhead Projection Device

PROCEDURE:

1. Create a template similar to the example (see Figure 2.1). Enter the vocabulary word in the main idea and title the surrounding ideas according to the following categories.

   • Syllables

   • Definitions

- Antonyms

- Synonyms

- Examples of the word in context

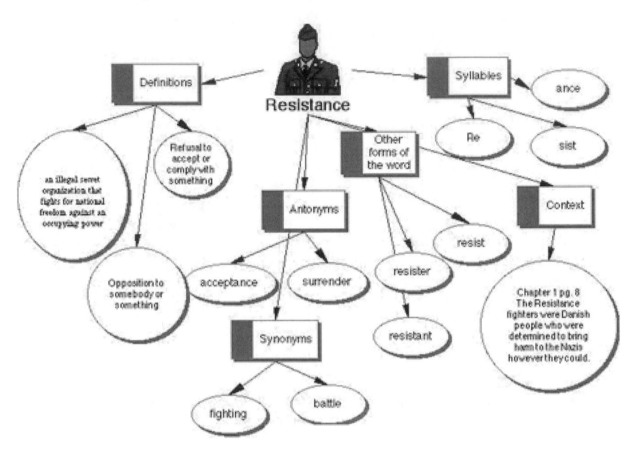

Figure 2.1 Completed word web

This diagram was created using Inspiration® by Inspiration Software®, Inc.

2. As students read their book, have them keep track of vocabulary words in a reading journal.

3. As a class, choose one vocabulary word to web in *Inspiration.* Explain to students that they will be dissecting the word using the dictionary.

4. Have students look up the word in the dictionary. Discuss the parts of a definition in the dictionary if students have little prior experience with dictionaries.

5. Add students' ideas to the categories already created (Syllables, Definitions, Antonyms, Synonyms, and Example of Word in Context). Use an overhead projection device if available.

6. Have all students complete their own word web using a word they gathered in their reading journal or from a read-aloud.

EXTENSIONS AND ADAPTATIONS:

- Younger students can do a general brainstorm of all the things they think of when they hear the word.

- Add other items to the word web such as pronunciation and part of speech.

ADDITIONAL RESOURCES:

Online Dictionaries:

Your Dictionary.com: **http://www.yourdictionary.com**
Merriam-Webster Online: **http://www.m-w.com/netdict.htm**
One-Look Dictionaries: **http://www.onelook.com**
Dictionary.com: **http://www.dictionary.com**

Vocabulary Slideshow

Swinburne, Stephen R. *Unbeatable Beaks.* Illustrated by Joan Paley. New York: Henry Holt and Company, 1999.

OVERVIEW:

Sometimes it is engaging and meaningful to listen to the way words sound in the book and to appreciate the author's choices. In this activity, students identify the words the author uses to describe things that birds do with their beaks. Then they create a slideshow of all those wonderful verbs!

GRADE LEVEL:

2–5

MATERIALS:

Slideshow Software *(Kid Pix Studio Deluxe, Powerpoint,* or *AppleWorks Slideshow)*

PROCEDURE:

1. Read *Unbeatable Beaks* to your students.

2. After the reading, discuss with your students the things that beaks can do. Make a list as a class (all words should be verbs).

3. Reread the book to the class and add to the list any new words.

   Your list might look like the following:

   Chisel

   Hook

   Pry

Preen

Slice

Scrape

Stab

Spike

Probe

Sip

Bite

Pick

Crack

Fight

4. Have students choose a verb from the list and create a rough draft of their slide away from the computer. Each slide should include a picture of the bird acting out the word, the vocabulary word, definition, and their name.

5. Next, have students create their slides in *Kid Pix* or another similar program (see Figure 2.2).

6. Put the slides together into a class slideshow. Add bird songs and sounds to each slide.

Figure 2.2 Illustration of verb

Taken from KidPix® Studio. ©Broderbund Properties LLC. Used with permission.

EXTENSIONS AND ADAPTATIONS:

- Add additional narrative to each slide from the book. For example, "A beak can pry, a beak can **preen,** the shape is straight, bent, in between."

- Look for other parts of speech in the book such as adjectives.

ADDITIONAL RESOURCES:

Kid Pix Walk-through in Appendix A

Kid Pix Planning Sheet Appendix B

Classroom Vocabulary Database

Fleischman, Sid. *The Whipping Boy.* New York: William Morrow and Co., 1987.

OVERVIEW:

A database serves as a great way to collect information and as a tool that is easy to search. By building a vocabulary database, you are creating an invaluable resource for yourself and your students.

GRADE LEVEL:

4–5

MATERIALS:

Database Software *(AppleWorks* or *Microsoft® Access)*

Drawing Software (Optional)

PROCEDURE:

1. Set up a database for the collection of vocabulary in your classroom (see Figure 2.3). Create fields for:

   - Vocabulary Word

   - Definition

   - Book Title

   - Chapter

   - Submitted by:

   - Picture (Optional)

   - Part of Speech (Optional)

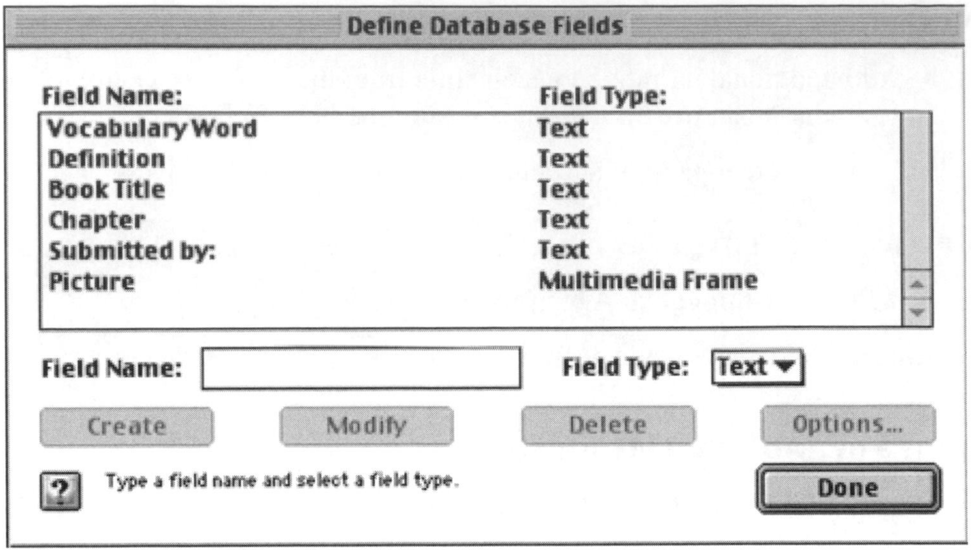

Figure 2.3 Window for defining details

2. Design a layout for student input (see Figure 2.4).

Figure 2.4 Sample record for one vocabulary word

3. Ask students to submit at least one word to the database each week. Students could also submit one word from each chapter they read. If you included a Picture field, have students insert their own graphic or a piece of clip-art.

4. Demonstrate how to sort the database by different fields. Sort the words by the field "Submitted by" to generate a list of one student's words to print out. Sort by book title if others are reading the same book and generate a larger list of words.

EXTENSIONS AND ADAPTATIONS:

- Create word lists, crossword puzzles, spelling lists, and other word-centered activities from the database. Try Discovery School's Puzzle Maker: **http://www.puzzlemaker.com**.

- Decrease the number of fields for younger students.

- Add other fields to the database such as a sentence field where the students can use the word in a sentence.

- Have each student write a question that can be answered using the database. Have students answer the questions as a class or individually.

ADDITIONAL RESOURCES:

Database Walk-through in Appendix A

Online Dictionaries:

Your Dictionary.com: **http://www.yourdictionary.com**
Merriam-Webster Online: **http://www.m-w.com/netdict.htm**
One-Look Dictionaries: **http://www.onelook.com**
Dictionary.com: **http://www.dictionary.com**

Visual Dictionary

Sachar, Louis. *Holes*. New York: Random House, Inc., 1998.

OVERVIEW:

One method of building vocabulary skills and helping students retain the meanings of words is to make a visual connection. Students will find the definitions of words and look for a piece of clip-art that relays that same meaning.

GRADE LEVEL:

3–5

MATERIALS:

Painting or drawing software *(AppleWorks* Drawing, *Kid Pix* or *Microsoft Word)*

Internet Access (Optional)

Visual Dictionary Planner Reproducible

Dictionary

Name_____ Date_____

Visual Dictionary Planner

1. Word _____ Picture_____

Definition_____

_____

2. Word _____ Picture_____

Definition_____

_____

3. Word _____ Picture_____

Definition_____

_____

4. Word _____ Picture_____

Definition_____

_____

5. Word _____ Picture_____

Definition_____

_____

6. Word _____ Picture_____

Definition_____

_____

7. Word _____ Picture_____

Definition_____

_____

8. Word _____ Picture_____

Definition_____

_____

Figure 2.5 Visual Dictionary Planner Reproducible

PROCEDURE:

1. Have students generate vocabulary words from the book they are reading using the worksheet provided. Students could generate words by choosing one from each chapter or selecting words from the most recent chapter that they read. You can also supply the vocabulary words (see Figure 2.5, the Visual Dictionary Planner).

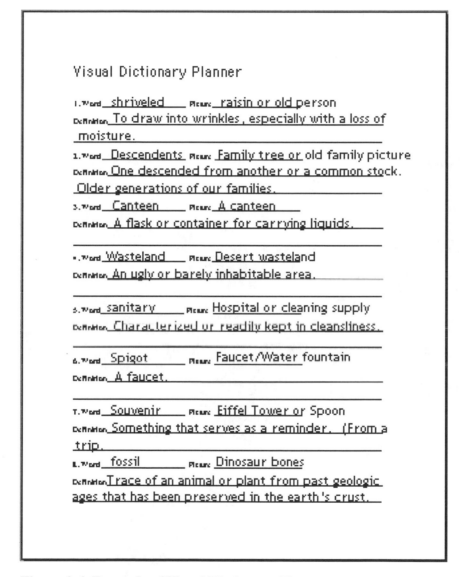

Visual Dictionary Planner

1. Word _shriveled_ Picture: _raisin or old person_
Definition: _To draw into wrinkles, especially with a loss of moisture._

2. Word _Descendents_ Picture: _Family tree or old family picture_
Definition: _One descended from another or a common stock. Older generations of our families._

3. Word _Canteen_ Picture: _A canteen_
Definition: _A flask or container for carrying liquids._

4. Word _Wasteland_ Picture: _Desert wasteland_
Definition: _An ugly or barely inhabitable area._

5. Word _sanitary_ Picture: _Hospital or cleaning supply_
Definition: _Characterized or readily kept in cleanliness._

6. Word _Spigot_ Picture: _Faucet/Water fountain_
Definition: _A faucet._

7. Word _Souvenir_ Picture: _Eiffel Tower or Spoon_
Definition: _Something that serves as a reminder. (From a trip._

8. Word _fossil_ Picture: _Dinosaur bones_
Definition: _Trace of an animal or plant from past geologic ages that has been preserved in the earth's crust._

Figure 2.6 Example of Visual Dictionary Planner

2. Next, have students obtain the definitions for the words.

3. Using the picture space provided on the worksheet (see Figure 2.6), ask students to brainstorm an image they are in search of. This will help refine their search when they are online.

4. Using free clip-art sites, search engines, or clip-art CDs, send students in search of clip-art that represents their vocabulary words. If students are using the Internet, refer them to the Appendix for the directions to grabbing an image from the Internet. Once they find an image, they can copy it from the Internet or CD and paste it into their drawing/painting program. Images can also be downloaded for later use in their collage.

5. Have students arrange the images in a visually pleasing way (see Figure 2.7). You may want students to incorporate the vocabulary words into their collage. Some students will be very linear and arrange the images in one column with the words in another while others may randomly place the images around the paper overlapping and rotating them. Allow for different styles.

Figure 2.7 Completed visual collage

6. Print out the collages and display them on the classroom bulletin board.

EXTENSIONS AND ADAPTATIONS:

- Younger students could choose only one word and illustrate it in a program like *Kid Pix*.

- If you have only one computer in your classroom, have each student visit the computer and be responsible for one vocabulary word and image in a classroom collage.

- Older students can take advantage of a great opportunity to learn how to properly cite images from the Internet. Have them type a bibliography to accompany their collage.

- If students are reading the same book, have them print their collages and swap with another classmate to try to match their vocabulary words to their images.

ADDITIONAL RESOURCES:

Copy/Paste and Online Clip-art Walk-through in Appendix A

Online Dictionaries:

Your Dictionary.com: **http://www.yourdictionary.com**
Merriam-Webster Online: **http://www.m-w.com/netdict.htm**
One-Look Dictionaries: **http://www.onelook.com**
Dictionary.com: **http://www.dictionary.com**

Clip-art Resources:

Google Image Surfer: **http://images.google.com**. This section of the Google Search site allows the user to search specifically for images. Type in a search word, and you will be presented with thumbnail images from a variety of Web sites.

ArtToday: **http://www.arttoday.com**. This site charges a fee based on how many weeks you sign up for the service. If you can afford to purchase a year subscription for your classroom, it would be worth the money. If not, consider purchasing a subscription for the length of time students will be working on a project that requires clip-art. The site is easy to navigate, and there is an endless amount of clip-art for almost any topic.

The Hyper Glossary

Macaulay, David. *Pyramid.* Boston: Houghton Mifflin Company, 1975.

OVERVIEW:

Many nonfiction books contain a glossary. Using a multimedia program, students will create a more in-depth glossary with pictures and hyperlinks that lead to additional information.

GRADE LEVEL:

3–5

MATERIALS:

Multimedia software *(Hyperstudio* or *Microsoft Powerpoint)*

Multimedia Planning Sheet Reproducible in Appendix B

PROCEDURE:

1. Discuss with your students why an author might include a glossary at the end of a book. In what types of books are glossaries usually found?

2. Read a book or section of a nonfiction book like *Pyramid* to your students. As you are reading, give them a copy of the glossary. When a word in the glossary is read aloud have them underline the word. If there is a word during the reading that they think should be on the glossary, but is not, have them add it to their page.

3. Discuss why students believe certain words are in the glossary.

4. Assign one word to individual students or a group of words to a small group. Explain to students that they will be creating a similar glossary using a multimedia program, but theirs will be more interactive.

5. Copy and distribute planning sheets to your students. Have students create a rough draft of their card or page using the Planning Sheet. Each page should include the word, a definition in their own words, and a visual representation.

6. Have students complete their glossary page on the computer (see Figure 2.8). They should also add a sound button or link that makes the word and/or definition be read aloud.

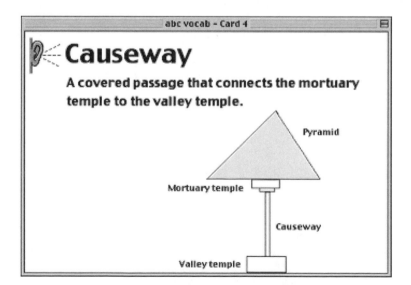

Figure 2.8 Completed glossary page
Hyperstudio® and all of its screen images are a registered trademark of Knowledge Adventure, Inc. and are used under license.

7. After students have completed their cards and sounds, create a title card for the glossary by typing a title and creating buttons or links for each letter of the alphabet (see Figure 2.9). Connect each letter of the alphabet to the students' completed cards. Last, students should revisit their glossary card and make a button or link to jump back to the title card.

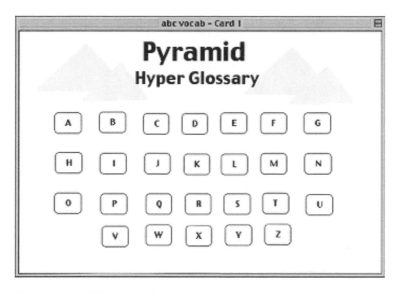

Figure 2.9 Title card for Hyper Glossary

Hyperstudio® and all of its screen images are a registered trademark of Knowledge Adventure, Inc. and are used under license.

EXTENSIONS AND ADAPTATIONS:

- Use the final glossary to assist with other related projects.

- Add other words to the glossary as students learn more from other sources.

- Add additional hyperlinks or buttons to the cards. In the example, the item *mortuary temple* could be linked to another card that contains the definition.

ADDITIONAL RESOURCE:

Hyperstudio Walk-through in Appendix A

CHAPTER 3

Genre

Each genre has specific features that define it. When we explore poetry, we examine the themes and meanings behind the words. With fiction, we focus on the literary elements of character, setting, and plot. In our classrooms, we need to examine the characteristics of the genre, talk about them, and read aloud from a variety of books. By familiarizing students with the different genres, we can encourage them to become more willing to try to read new genres on their own, and when students study the elements in-depth, they can try new forms of writing with more confidence. Technology can guide us to activities that make the most of the specific genre. Some activities in this chapter will lead readers to understand the specific conventions of a genre whereas others will help students to see the differences. At the end of the chapter there is a section titled Other Genre Ideas. Here you will find brief descriptions of activities that fit specific genres as well as references to other chapters with activities that may apply to the genre you are teaching.

Diagramming a Genre

Perrault, Charles. *Cinderella.* Retold by Amy Ehrlich. Illustrated by Susan Jeffers. New York: Dial Books for Young Readers, 1985.

OVERVIEW:

Dissecting a genre can help students understand the qualities of the stories they read as well as contribute to their own writing. Use a diagramming program like *Inspiration* to brainstorm the specific qualities of one genre.

GRADE LEVEL:

1–5

MATERIALS:

Inspiration Software

Overhead Projection Device

PROCEDURE:

1. When students have had sufficient time to acquaint themselves with the chosen genre, explain to them that they will be brainstorming what makes the genre unique and different from others.

2. Open *Inspiration* and begin by placing the words "Fairy Tales and Folk Tales" in the main idea in the middle of the screen. Below this idea, create three more ideas to categorize elements of the setting, characters, and themes that are characteristic of this genre. To encourage class participation, connect your computer to a larger screen with an overhead projection device.

3. Ask students to contribute characteristics of the specific genre that fall within these categories. With each characteristic that students contribute, add another bubble to the screen. Connect the bubbles to the category they belong to and if you prefer, go in order starting with common settings in Fairy Tales and Folk Tales (see Figure 3.1).

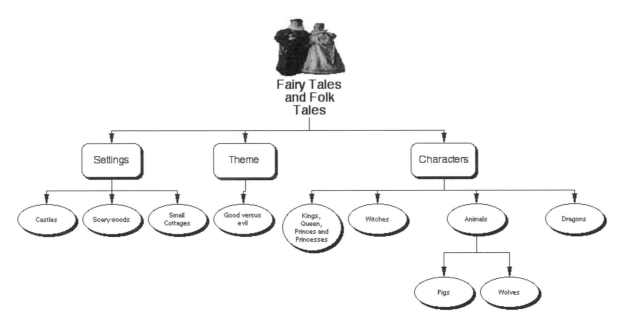

Figure 3.1 Completed genre diagram

This diagram was created using Inspiration® by Inspiration Software®, Inc.

4. Choose a book from this genre like *Cinderella* and check to see which characteristics apply to the brainstorm. Add notes to the setting, theme, and character ideas to describe what these elements look like in the specific story (see Figure 3.2). Notes can be added to ideas by clicking on the idea and selecting the "Add Note" button at the top of the screen.

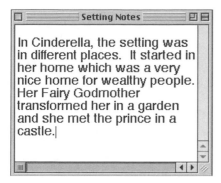

Figure 3.2 Setting notes from the genre diagram

EXTENSIONS AND ADAPTATIONS:

- Have students use the genre diagram created by the class to compare it to a book they have read from the same genre.

- Try creating genre diagrams for each different genre. Are there similarities or differences? Post the diagrams in your classroom for students to refer to.

- Compare and contrast two books from the same genre. How close are their characteristics? Create a Venn diagram displaying the similarities and differences.

- Have your students write a story based on the elements of this specific genre. Have them use the diagram to make sure they have covered all necessary aspects.

ADDITIONAL RESOURCE:

Inspiration Walk-through in Appendix A

The Great Genre Tree

Lord, Bette Bao. *In the Year of the Boar and Jackie Robinson.* Illustrated by Marc Simont. New York: Harper and Row, 1984.

OVERVIEW:

To familiarize your students with the different genres, brainstorm genres using a graphic organizer and with the Notes feature of *Inspiration,* add an additional level of information to each genre.

GRADE LEVEL:

3–5

MATERIALS:

Inspiration Software

Overhead Projection Device

Procedure:

1. Open *Inspiration* and begin by placing the word "Genre" in the main idea in the middle of the screen. Explain to students that they will be brainstorming the different genres. To encourage class participation, connect your computer to a larger screen with an overhead projection device.

2. With each genre that students contribute, add another bubble to the screen.

3. When the brainstorming is done, ideas should be scattered all over the screen. Add any genres that were not considered by students and link all the specific genres to the main idea (see Figure 3.3).

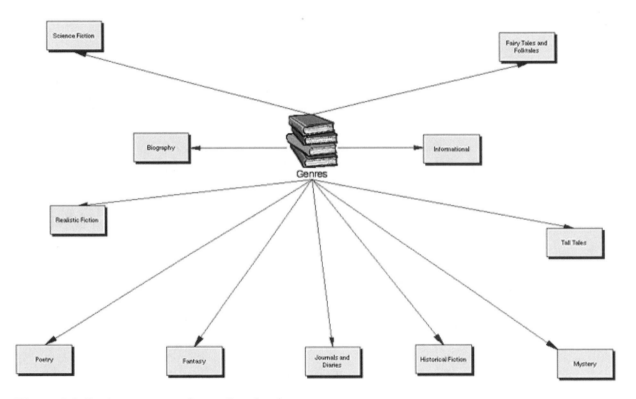

Figure 3.3 Basic genre tree from class brainstorm

This diagram was created using Inspiration® by Inspiration Software®, Inc.

4. Save the file for later use by students.

5. Divide your class into groups for each genre.

6. Assign each group the task of finding three books from the genre that they might be interested in reading or have already read.

7. Next, have each group read at least one new book from the genre.

8. Using the original diagram, have each group add the books they have read to their assigned genre by creating individual ideas for each book and linking the book titles ideas to the genre ideas (see Figure 3.4).

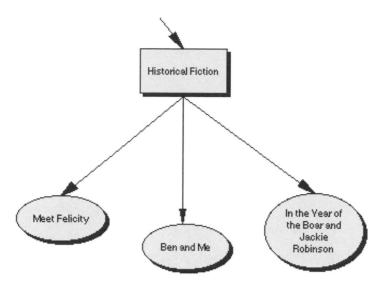

Figure 3.4 Example of book titles added to one genre bubble

This diagram was created using Inspiration® by Inspiration Software®, Inc.

9. Using the Notes feature, have students add a note to each book that includes the Title, Author, Illustrator, and a Quick Summary. Notes can be added to ideas by clicking on the idea and selecting the "Add Note" button at the top of the screen (see Figure 3.5). A picture can be added by copying from one program and pasting into the Notes section.

Figure 3.5 Notes added to a book bubble

10. After the diagram is finished, have students peruse the selections that other groups added. Students can also use the diagram to make future book selections.

EXTENSIONS AND ADAPTATIONS:

- Turn the diagram into a game by removing the links from the books to the genre ideas and mixing the book titles around the screen. Students could visit the computer and try to match the book to the genre by linking them again. The Notes section would be helpful in identifying the type of book.

- Create Internet hyperlinks that link to Web sites related to the book. For example, a Harry Potter book could link to the Harry Potter section of the Scholastic Web site (look under the Utility menu).

- Create a genre tree for read-alouds throughout the year or have students keep a record of their independent reading selections by creating their own genre tree.

- Download pictures of the book covers from a bookstore Web site and add these to the Symbol Palette (look under the Utility menu). Then change the Ideas symbol to the actual book covers.

ADDITIONAL RESOURCE:

Inspiration Walk-through in Appendix A

Literary Genre Log

Mado, Michio. *The Animals*. Translated by The Empress Michiko of Japan. Illustrated by Mitsumasa Anno. New York: Macmillan Publishing Company, 1992.

OVERVIEW:

A database or "literary log" will allow students to quickly and briefly keep track of their personal reading selections. More traditionally, a reading log is kept in a reading journal or notebook. If students are allowed to input their books into a database, though, they can search and sort to learn more about their reading preferences.

GRADE LEVEL:

3–5

MATERIALS:

Database Software *(AppleWorks* or *Microsoft Access)*

Drawing Software (Optional)

PROCEDURE:

1. Set up a database for students to keep track of the books they have read (see Figure 3.6). Create fields for:

   - Book Title

   - Author

   - Illustrator (if any)

   - Genre

   - Rating (5, 4, 3, 2, 1)

   - Comments:

   - Submitted by:

   - Picture (Optional)

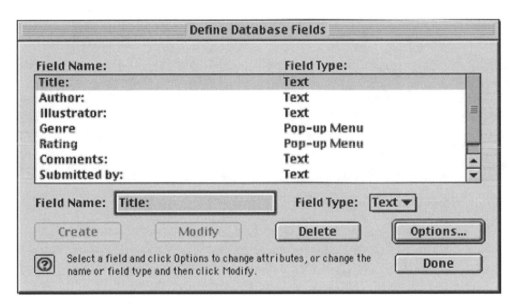

Figure 3.6 Window for defining fields

2. Design a layout for student input (see Figure 3.7).

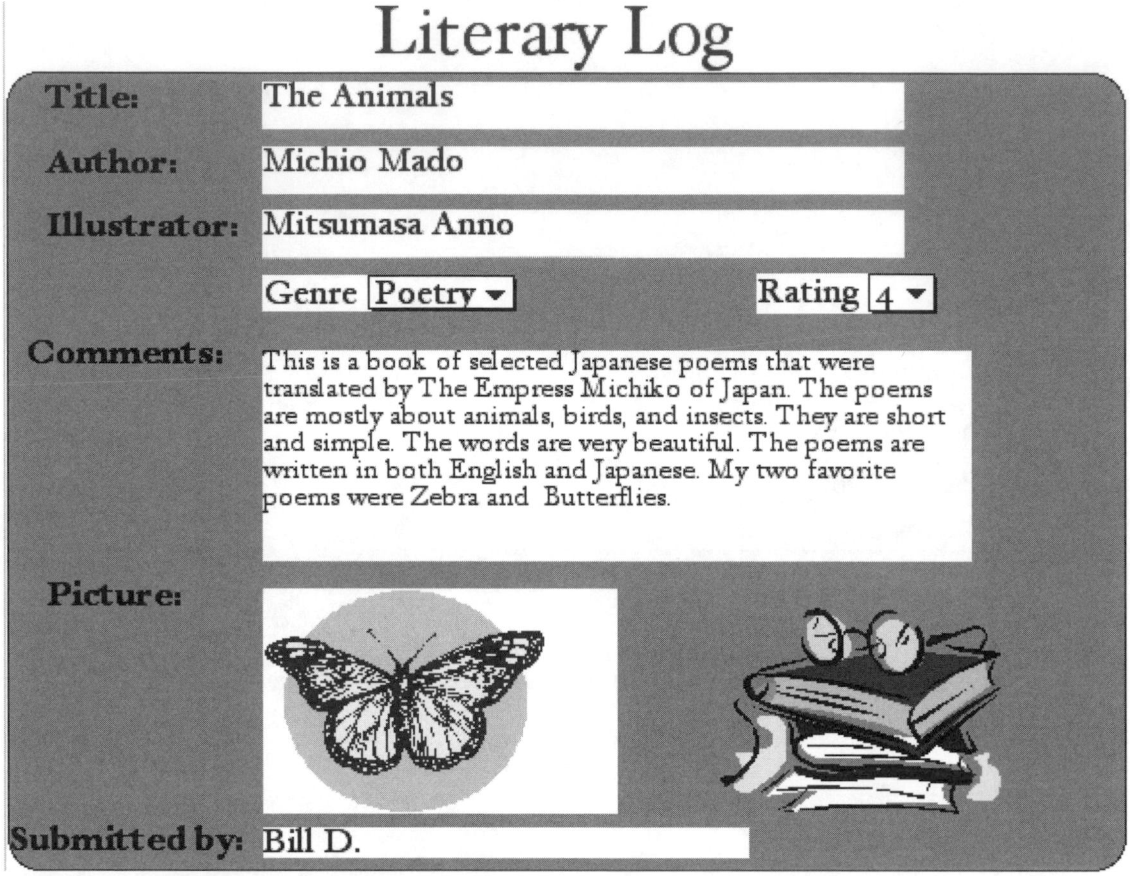

Literary Log

Title: The Animals

Author: Michio Mado

Illustrator: Mitsumasa Anno

Genre Poetry ▼   Rating 4 ▼

Comments: This is a book of selected Japanese poems that were translated by The Empress Michiko of Japan. The poems are mostly about animals, birds, and insects. They are short and simple. The words are very beautiful. The poems are written in both English and Japanese. My two favorite poems were Zebra and Butterflies.

Picture:

Submitted by: Bill D.

Figure 3.7 Sample record for one book

3. Ask students to create an entry in their database each time they complete an independent reading selection. If students wish, they could also maintain a list in their reading journals and transfer the information to the database once every couple of weeks. If the database contains a picture field, have students insert their own graphic or clip-art that symbolizes the book.

4. Demonstrate how to conduct a "find" and how to "sort" the database by different fields. Conduct a find with the field "Genre" to generate a list of books from a specific genre. Ask students to look at the genres they have read at different times throughout the year. If there is a genre they have not tried, ask them to choose a book from that genre to read. Conduct other finds and sorts to show students the potential of collecting reading data in a database. Sort by author, and see if there are any authors who write in multiple genres.

EXTENSIONS AND ADAPTATIONS:

- Create a basic database template with the fields you desire and have students create their own database layouts to personalize their logs.

- At the end of the school year, have students use their databases to find books from each genre that they consider to be the best. Have students print out records to vote for the best book within a genre.

- Change the format of the template for different grade levels. Increase fields for upper grades and decrease for lower grades. Enlarge fonts and field sizes in the layout for younger students.

- Create a Columnar Report layout for simple printing purposes. Have students print their lists at the end of each quarter or trimester.

- Do a find using two categories such as a five rating and the Science Fiction/Fantasy genre. This will generate a list of the top books from the Science Fiction/ Fantasy category.

- Print out a blank record for students to complete away from the computer. Later, they can use the record to input the information into the database, or if computer time is limited, designate a specific student or parent volunteer who is responsible each week for inputting other students' records.

- Have your students assist in designing the database by brainstorming what fields should be created. This is a great critical thinking skill because students will need to think about the ways in which they will want to sort the database later. This is also a great introduction to databases.

- Have all your students contribute to one class database so there are more books to search through.

- Build a book database for your own personal teaching library.

ADDITIONAL RESOURCE:

Database Walk-through in Appendix A

Diagramming a Mystery

Sobel, Donald. *Encyclopedia Brown Takes the Case.* Illustrated by Leonard Shortall. New York: Elsevier-Dutton Publishing Company, Inc., 1973.

OVERVIEW:

Use *Inspiration* to solve a mystery and to better understand the elements in the mystery genre.

GRADE LEVEL:

2–5

MATERIALS:

Inspiration Software

Overhead Projection Device (Optional)

PROCEDURE:

1. Create a template similar to the following example (see Figure 3.8). First, create a text box at the top of the diagram using the Text tool. Leave room for students to enter the title and author. Below the text box, create three ideas that go across the page horizontally. Enter "Suspects" in the first one, "The Facts" in the second, and "Encyclopedia's Conclusions" or simply "Conclusions" in the last. (In the case of Encyclopedia Brown, the conclusion category was broken into two connecting ideas. The first was for Encyclopedia's conclusion and the second for why he came to that conclusion. This characteristic is unique to the Encyclopedia Brown series so modify your template according to the book you are using.) Link these three ideas to each other and create more empty ideas that connect to each of the three main ideas. In the example, clip-art was chosen from the Symbol Palette to represent the categories of suspects, facts, and conclusions.

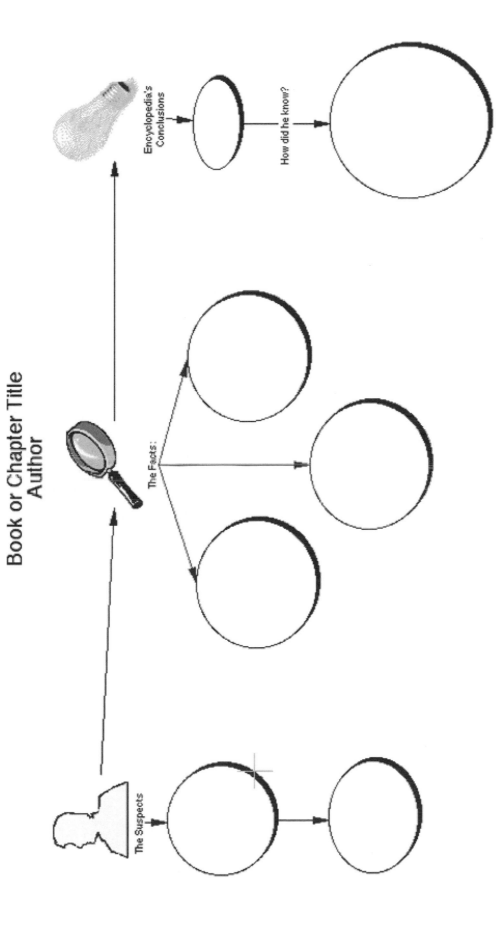

Figure 3.8 Template of mystery diagram

This diagram was created using Inspiration® by Inspiration Software®. Inc.

2. Read aloud one chapter from *Encyclopedia Brown Takes the Case* by Donald Sobel. Each chapter in this series of mystery books details a simple crime case that is quickly solved.

3. After reading the chapter to your students, open the template. With your students, fill in the bubbles according to the facts in the story. In the "How did he know?" bubble generate students' predictions about how Encyclopedia solved the case (see Figure 3.9).

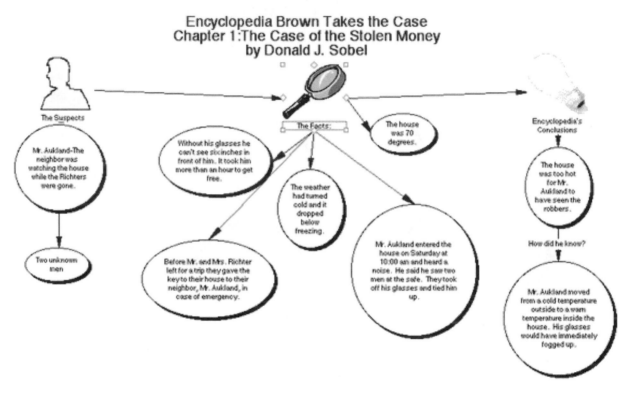

Figure 3.9 Completed mystery diagram
This diagram was created using Inspiration® by Inspiration Software®, Inc.

4. Have students read an Encyclopedia case or another mystery book and then fill in the template on their own.

EXTENSIONS AND ADAPTATIONS:

*   Using the template, have students plan and then write their own mysteries.

*   Add other ideas to the brainstorm such as further details about where the crime took place or additional information about the suspects.

ADDITIONAL RESOURCES:

Inspiration Walk-through in Appendix A

Other Mystery Books (Each of these books is part of a series.)

Adler, David A. *Cam Jansen and the Mystery of the Gold Coins.* Illustrated by Susanna Natti. New York: Viking Penguin, 1982.

Landon, Lucinda. *Meg Mackintosh and the Mystery at Camp Creepy.* North Scituate, RI: Secret Passage Press, 1990.

Osbourne, Mary Pope. *Mystery under the May-Apple.* New York: Random House Inc., 1992.

Interpreting Poetry with a Word Processor

Koch, Kenneth, and Kate Farrell. *Talking to the Sun.* New York: The Metropolitan Museum of Art, 1985.

OVERVIEW:

Poetry brings feelings and images to our minds. In this activity, students transform the text of a poem by changing the fonts, sizes, and styles to reflect the feelings and images they find in the words.

GRADE LEVEL:

3–5

MATERIALS:

Word Processing Software *(AppleWorks* or *Microsoft Word)*

Overhead Projection Device

PROCEDURE:

1. Choose a poem that has several themes or meanings that students can discuss aloud. Type the poem into a word processing program and save the poem for later use by students.

   I Wandered Lonely as a Cloud

   I wandered lonely as a cloud
   That floats on high o'er vales and hills,
   When all at once I saw a crowd,
   A host, of golden daffodils;
   Beside the lake, beneath the trees,
   Fluttering and dancing in the breeze.

   Continuous as the stars that shine
   And twinkle on the milky way,
   They stretched in never-ending line
   Along the margin of a bay:
   Ten thousand saw I at a glance,
   Tossing their heads in sprightly dance.

The waves beside them danced; but
   they
Out-did the sparkling waves in glee:
A poet could not but be gay,
In such a jocund company:
I gazed—and gazed—but little thought
What wealth the show to me had
   Brought:

For oft, when on my couch I lie
In vacant or in pensive mood,
They flash upon that inward eye
Which is the bliss of solitude;
And then my heart with pleasure fills,
And dances with the daffodils.

William Wordsworth, 1770–1850

2. Display the poem using an overhead projection device connected to your computer.

3. Discuss the poem's meaning with students. Have them think about the meanings of particular words and phrases. What items stand out? What lines or phrases do they like the sound of? Reread the poem several times to give students a chance to think about the meaning and hear the words.

4. Explain to students that sometimes authors can change the look of a poem by placing certain words on certain lines or making a word bold so it stands out from the rest of the words. Using the different fonts, sizes, styles, and colors select a couple of phrases or words in the poem to change based on student interpretations.

5. Allow students to work independently with their own file to change the poem based on their own interpretations (see Figure 3.10).

6. Have students print out their transformed poetry.

I Wandered Lonely as a **CLOUD**

I wandered lonely as a **CLOUD**
That floats on high o'er vales and hills,
When all at once I saw a crowd,
A host, of golden daffodils;
Beside the lake, beneath the trees,
Fluttering and *dancing* in the breeze.

Continuous as the stars that **SHINE**
And **TWINKLE** on the milky way,
They stretched in never-ending l i n e
Along the margin of a bay:
Ten thousand saw I at a glance,
Tossing their heads in *sprightly dance.*

The waves beside them *danced*; but
 they
Out-did the **SPARKLING** waves in glee:
A poet could not but be *gay*,
In such a *jocund* company:
I gazed-and gazed-but little thought
What wealth the show to me had
 brought:

For oft, when on my couch I lie
In vacant or in pensive mood,
They **FLASH** upon that inward eye
Which is the *bliss* of solitude;
And then my heart with pleasure **fills**,
And *dances* with the daffodils.

                    William Wordsworth, 1770-1850

Figure 3.10 Interpreted poetry through a word processor

EXTENSIONS AND ADAPTATIONS:

- Allow students to choose their own poems to bring alive with fonts, sizes, colors, and styles.

- Discuss which words students chose to highlight and why? How did they choose to transform the words? Did they simply make it bold or did they change the font? Were there any words that were difficult to change even though the word had importance?

- Add clip-art next to the poem or incorporate a background image.

ADDITIONAL RESOURCES:

Prelutsky, Jack. *The 20th Century Children's Poetry Treasury.* Illustrated by Meilo So. New York: Alfred A. Knopf, 1999.

Other Genre Ideas

Diaries

If students are reading diaries, have them create their own multimedia diaries with a word processing program or multimedia program like *Hyperstudio.* Scholastic also publishes a program called *Diary Maker* that contains three famous diaries from Zlata Filipovic, Anne Frank, and Latoya Hunter. It also includes a password-protected diary where students can create entries and personalize their writing with sticky notes and audio clips.

Fairy Tales

Search for fairy tales on the Internet. Because these stories are typically out of print, they are free from several Web sites. See the activity "Using Online Literature" in Chapter 5 to find more resources and Web sites.

Realistic Fiction

- When students read realistic fiction they have the opportunity to connect with the characters because the events in the book may be similar to their own. See the activity "Connecting with the Text" in Chapter 7.

- All types of fiction have the common elements of character, setting, and plot. See Chapter 1 for more activities that focus on these elements.

Picture Books

If you want your students to learn more about the picture book format, have them create their own picture books using word processing software or storybook software.

Historical Fiction

This genre presents the opportunity for students to create timelines of the events surrounding whatever historical era the book may be about. Use a program like *Time-Liner 5.0* by Tom Snyder Software.

Animals

- If students enjoy books about animals, have them go online and do research about an animal in the book they are reading.

- Try a field trip to an online zoo to allow students to learn more about their animals.

Autobiography and Biography

Use the Internet to conduct research on the selected person. The Internet can be a very valuable tool because up-to-date information can be found.

A&E's Biography Web site: **http://www.biography.com**

Nonfiction

Some informational books contain charts or graphs to represent information pictorially. Have students create a chart using a spreadsheet program to accompany an informational book they are reading.

Fantasy or Mythology

- Have students explore the various characters in the fantasy or mythology genre using the Encyclopedia Mythica, an online encyclopedia that contains both mythological beings as well as fantasy characters like elves, ogres, and centaurs. After locating the definition, have students print the page from the Internet and use a drawing program to draw a picture and type the definition.

The Encyclopedia Mythica: **http://www.pantheon.org/mythica.html**

- Have students use a poster or drawing program to create a wanted poster for a mythological or fantasy character.

Poetry

- Have your students try writing their own poetry using an online Magnetic Poetry site.

Magnetic Word Poetry Web site: **http://www.shadowpoetry.com/magnet.html**

- Refer to "Creating an Interactive Poetry Book" activity in Chapter 6. This activity uses poetry in the example.

Book Reports

Traditionally, a book report is a written report that follows a specific format which may possibly summarize the story or include a student's personal reflections. Some educators prefer to call today's book report a "response to literature." This response can be completed artistically, orally, or in writing. The purpose of a book report can be to check for student understanding and comprehension but more importantly to ascertain what the student learned or brought away from the reading experience. Technology offers you and students more alternatives to the traditional book report while also providing incentive and motivation.

Chapter-by-Chapter Slideshow

MacLachlan, Patricia. *Sarah, Plain and Tall.* New York: HarperCollins Publishers, 1985.

OVERVIEW:

A book report doesn't have to be completed by just one student. Extend a read-aloud by asking students to illustrate each chapter on the computer. When the book is finished and the pictures are completed, organize the student pictures into a chapter-by-chapter slideshow.

GRADE LEVEL:

K–5

MATERIALS:

Painting and Slideshow Software *(Kid Pix Studio Deluxe)*

PROCEDURE:

1. Explain to students that they will be creating a slideshow of the important events in the book.

2. Before you begin the read-aloud, draw names or assign a chapter to each student. If the book you are reading has too few chapters, have students pair up to complete their pictures or have two students draw two separate pictures for the slideshow.

71

Figure 4.1 Illustration of event in Chapter 5
Taken from Kid Pix® Studio. ©Broderbund Properties LLC. Used with permission.

3. As you read, have a designated student jot down notes so the students can remember what events occurred in the chapter, or at the end of each chapter discuss with students what events or moments stood out in their minds.

4. Have a designated student draw his or her picture of one event or moment from the chapter on the computer (see Figure 4.1). This could be done during reading time or during the next day's read-aloud.

5. When all pictures are completed, assemble the slideshow using the slideshow feature in *Kid Pix Studio Deluxe* (see Figure 4.2). Don't forget to have one student create a title slide.

EXTENSIONS AND ADAPTATIONS:

*   If your school has a scanner, students can draw their pictures away from the computer and scan them for the slideshow.

*   Have individual students create their own chapter-by-chapter slideshows.

ADDITIONAL RESOURCES:

Kid Pix Walk-through in Appendix A

Kid Pix Planning Sheet in Appendix B

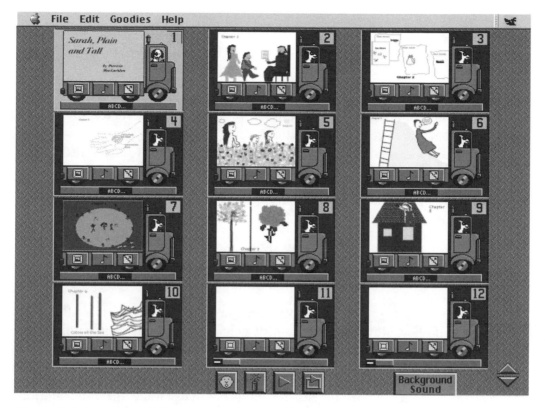

Figure 4.2 Completed chapter-by-chapter slideshow
Taken from Kid Pix® Studio. ©Broderbund Properties LLC. Used with permission.

Multimedia Report

Mowatt, Farley. *Owls in the Family.* Boston: Little, Brown and Company, 1962.

OVERVIEW:

Multimedia software allows students to create highly visual, interactive reports, and using an overhead projection device, students can share their final products with the rest of their classmates.

GRADE LEVEL:

2–5

MATERIALS:

Multimedia or Slideshow Software *(Hyperstudio, Kid Pix Slideshow, AppleWorks* or *Microsoft Powerpoint)*

Multimedia Book Report Guidelines Reproducibles (Either the guidelines used for the example [see Figure 4.3] or the generic guidelines that can be filled in [see Figure 4.4].)

Multimedia Planning Sheet Reproducible in Appendix B

Multimedia Rubric Reproducible in Appendix B

Overhead Projection Device

PROCEDURE:

1. Have your students self-select a book for the project. Create guidelines for their multimedia book reports using the generic guidelines by writing in each box what you would like students to place on each card or slide. You can also use the guidelines used in the example from *Owls in the Family.*

2. Distribute and share the **Multimedia Book Report Guidelines** and the **Multimedia Rubric** with your students.

3. Have students complete planning sheets for each slide before working on the computer. Planning sheets minimize time spent on the computer and allow students to do the necessary editing on a rough draft.

4. Using the desired program, demonstrate how students will assemble their information into a slideshow. Review any necessary technology skills that students must have. Give students adequate time to complete their book reports on the computer. (Students will need four to six 45-minute time blocks.) (See Figures 4.5, 4.6, 4.7, 4.8, 4.9, and 4.10.)

5. Set up a schedule for student presentations. Distribute the presentations over a week's time. Draw names or assign dates and times to each student. On the **Multimedia Report Guidelines** reproducible, there is a space to write in the due date for each student.

6. As students share their book reports, evaluate them using the **Multimedia Rubric** found in the Appendix.

EXTENSIONS AND ADAPTATIONS:

- Have students add sounds or animations to their book reports.

- Increase or decrease the amount of required cards or slides based on their grade level and your expectations.

- Leave the requirements open to students and see where their creativity takes them.

- *Inspiration* software can be valuable when planning a multimedia report. Have students use the program to plan how their stack will be structured.

ADDITIONAL RESOURCES:

Hyperstudio Walk-through in the Appendix A

Web Sites:

The Great Horned Owl Webquest: **http://www.qesn.meq.gouv.qc.ca/schools/pcartier/owlquest.htm**

Teacher CyberGuide for Owls in the Family: **http://www.sdcoe.k12.ca.us/score/owl/owltg.htm**

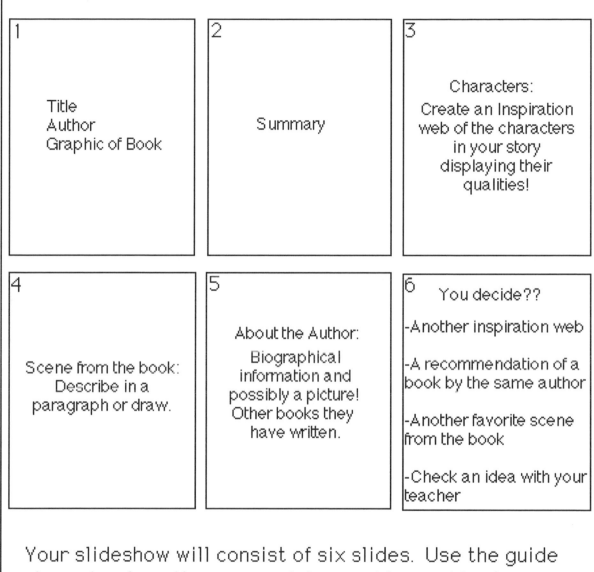

Multimedia Book Report Guidelines

1	2	3
Title Author Graphic of Book	Summary	Characters: Create an Inspiration web of the characters in your story displaying their qualities!

4	5	6 You decide??
Scene from the book: Describe in a paragraph or draw.	About the Author: Biographical information and possibly a picture! Other books they have written.	-Another inspiration web -A recommendation of a book by the same author -Another favorite scene from the book -Check an idea with your teacher

Your slideshow will consist of six slides. Use the guide above to place the appropriate graphics and text on each page. When your work is completed, use the Multimedia Rubric to evaluate your work. Be prepared to share your slideshow by_____.

Figure 4.3 Example guidelines

Multimedia Book Report Guidelines

1	2	3

4	5	6

Your slideshow will consist of six slides. Use the guide above to place the appropriate graphics and text on each page. When your work is completed, use the Multimedia Rubric to evaluate your work. Be prepared to share your slideshow by_____.

Figure 4.4 Template for creating your own guidelines

Figure 4.5 Title slide

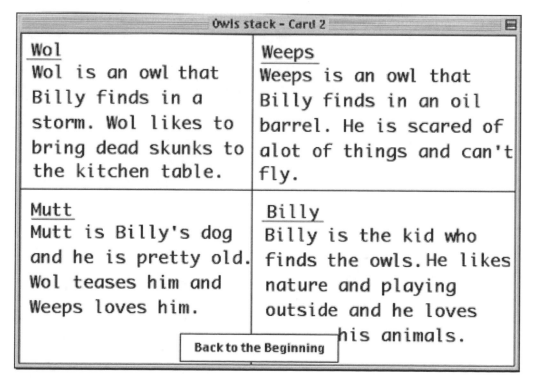

Figure 4.6 "About the characters" slide

Hyperstudio® and all of its screen images are a registered trademark of Knowledge Adventure, Inc. and are used under license.

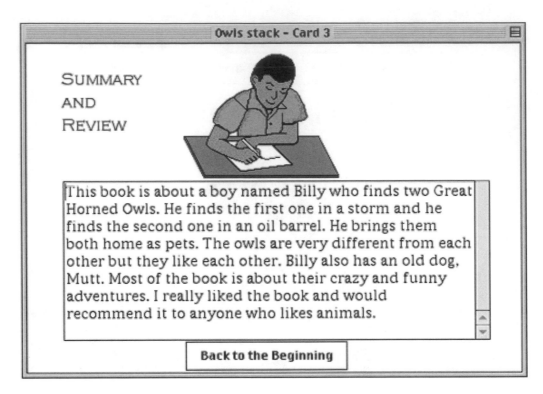

Figure 4.7 Summary slide

Figure 4.8 "Scene from the book" slide

Hyperstudio® and all of its screen images are a registered trademark of Knowledge Adventure, Inc. and are used under license.

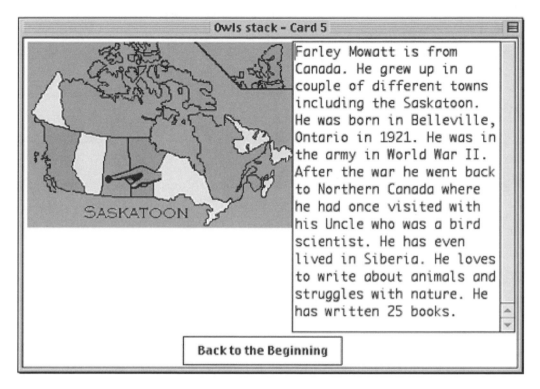

Figure 4.9 "About the author" slide

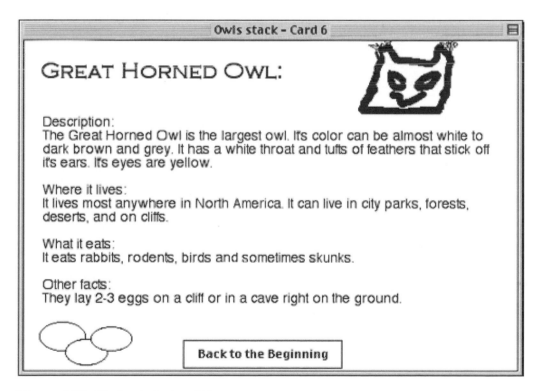

Figure 4.10 Student choice slide

Hyperstudio® and all of its screen images are a registered trademark of Knowledge Adventure, Inc. and are used under license.

Webbing a Report

Le Guin, Ursula K. *Catwings.* Illustrated by S. D. Schindler. New York: Scholastic Inc., 1988.

OVERVIEW:

Although *Inspiration* is used primarily for brainstorming and diagramming various concepts, it can also be used to diagram a book report and can serve as a "container" for additional information.

GRADE LEVEL:

2–5

MATERIALS:

Inspiration Software

Overhead Projection Device

PROCEDURE:

1. Create a story map similar to the diagram shown in Figure 4.11. Save the file to be used later by students.

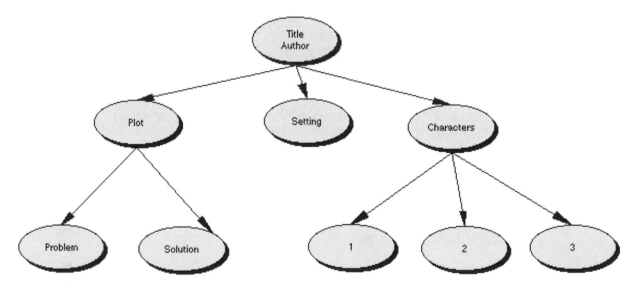

Figure 4.11 Story map template
This diagram was created using Inspiration® by Inspiration Software®, Inc.

2. Introduce students to the story map you created in *Inspiration.* Demonstrate how to change the main ideas text to the title and author of a book that your students are familiar with. Leave the Setting, Plot, Problem, Solution, and Character ideas

alone. Last, change the ideas attached to Character to the names of the main characters in the book (see Figure 4.12). Add additional ideas if necessary.

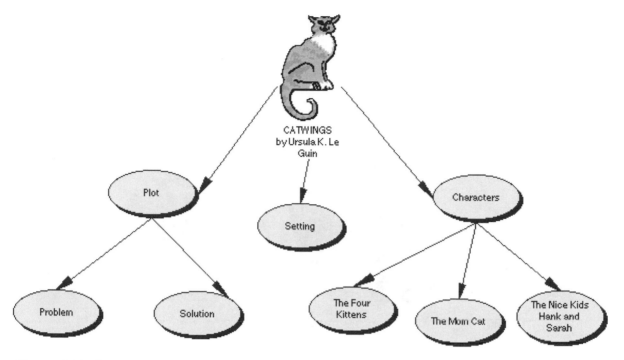

Figure 4.12 Completed story map

This diagram was created using Inspiration® by Inspiration Software®, Inc.

3. Using the Notes feature, add notes to the problem and solution ideas giving further
details about the story's plot. Next, add notes to the character ideas describing each
character (see Figure 4.13). Because you are modeling the procedure, keep your
notes brief. Notes can be added to ideas by clicking on the idea and selecting the
"Add Note" button at the top of the screen.

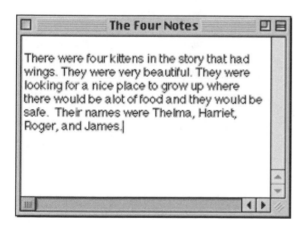

Figure 4.13 Character Notes

4. Add a note to the setting. In the setting notes instead of typing a description, add a picture by copying from a drawing program and pasting into the Notes section (see Figure 4.14).

The cats lived in an alley with lots of trash.

Figure 4.14 Setting Notes with a pasted graphic

5. In the main idea that holds the title and author information; add a note that gives your personal opinion about the book.

6. Finally, show students what the diagram looks like in the Outline format (see Figure 4.15). In Outline format the notes will all be visible.

⊙ CATWINGS

by Ursula K. Le Guin

I liked this book. I could read it fast. I wish we knew more about what happened to the cats once they found a good home in the barn. There should be a sequel to this book.

I. + Plot

A. = Problem

The four cats with wings lived in a bad neighborhood where there was not a lot of food. It was not very safe. Their mom wanted them to be safer. She knew that their wings could help them get away.

B. = Solution

Their mom told them to use their wings to fly away to a better place. They went to the woods. This was not the best place to be because the owls tried to hunt them but then one day they found a very nice little girl. She had a friend and they decided to let the cats live in the barn where other people would not see them because adults might put them in a special zoo because they were so different.

II. = Setting

The cats lived in an alley with lots of trash.

III. + Characters

A. = The Four Kittens

There were four kittens in the story that had wings. They were very beautiful. They were looking for a nice place to grow up where there would be a lot of food and they would be safe. Their names were Thelma, Harriet, Roger, and James.

B. = The Mom Cat

Mrs. Jane Tabby had a dream that she could fly away from her neighborhood. She thought that might be the reason why she had four kittens with wings. She cared very much about her kittens so she asked them to leave. She was about to start a new family with Mr. Tom Jones.

C. = The Nice Kids

Hank and Sarah

Sarah saw one of the kittens so she brought food to it. She thought the kitten was very beautiful. The next day she brought her friend Hank and more food. All the kittens came. Sarah and Frank decided that they would find a good place for the kittens to live and be safe.

Figure 4.15 Diagram in outline format

7. Have students create their own *Inspiration* book reports with their own reading selections.

8. When their reports are finished, have students print out their report in both the Diagram and Outline format.

EXTENSIONS AND ADAPTATIONS:

- For younger students, have them fill in the basic story map with the simple details from their story and print the diagram out.

- Have students include a drawing in each note.

- Allow students to change the ideas to other graphics in the Symbol Palette that are specific to the book they read.

- Include other ideas in the diagram such as theme or information about the author.

ADDITIONAL RESOURCES:

Inspiration Walk-through in Appendix A

Copy/Paste and Online Clip-art Walk-through in Appendix A

Database Book Reports

Levine, Gail Carson. *Ella Enchanted.* New York: HarperCollins Publishers Inc., 1997.

OVERVIEW:

A database can be used for student book reports by creating a template that students are required to fill in after they finish a reading selection. You create the format, and the student types in the required information. Later, the database can be used by other students to search for new book selections.

GRADE LEVEL:

3–5

MATERIALS:

Database Software *(AppleWorks* or *Microsoft Access)*

PROCEDURE:

1. Setup a database for a student book report. Create fields for:

   - Book Title

   - Author

   - Illustrator (if any)

   - Write a brief summary of the book:

   - Tell me about the main character:

   - Where did the book take place?

   - Would you recommend this book to anyone else? Why or why not?

   - Submitted by (see Figure 4.16):

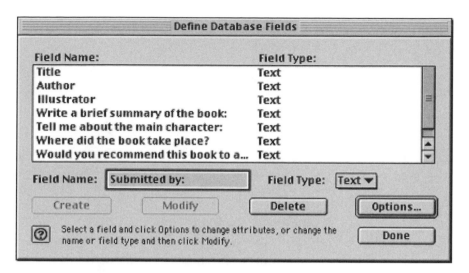

Figure 4.16 Window for defining fields

2. Design a layout for student input (see Figure 4.17).

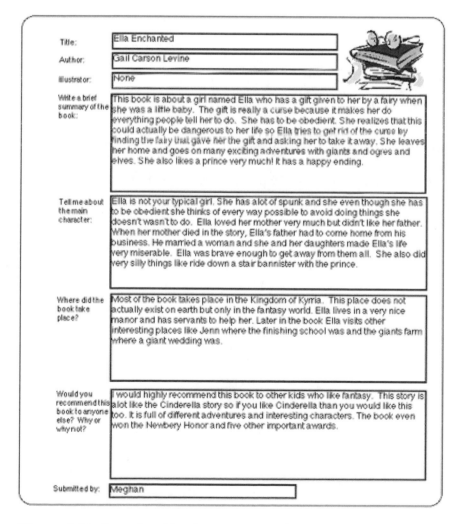

Figure 4.17 Completed book report record

3. Require students to complete one book report during the semester or school year using the book report database.

4. After students have typed in the necessary information, they should print out their record.

EXTENSIONS AND ADAPTATIONS:

- Print a blank record for students to complete away from the computer. This can be their rough draft. Later, they can use the draft to input the information into the database.

- If you have already set up a database similar to the "Classroom Vocabulary Database" in Chapter 2 or the "Literary Genre Log" in Chapter 3, then use the same database for book reports. Add new fields to the other databases and insert these fields into a new layout. (A database can have many fields, but each layout does not have to include each one of the fields.)

- Change the fields based on your own book report requirements or based on a specific genre your class is reading.

- Encourage students to search the database when they are looking for a new book.

ADDITIONAL RESOURCE:

Database Walk-through in Appendix A

Extra! Extra! Read All About It!

Crilley, Mark. *Akiko on the Planet Smoo.* New York: Random House Inc., 2000.

OVERVIEW:

A newsletter provides students with a creative response to the special events and characters in a book. In this activity, four students create a newsletter from a book they have finished reading as a group. When all the students have contributed an article to you, they then create the newsletter using a word processing program.

GRADE LEVEL:

3–5

MATERIALS:

Word Processing Software *(AppleWorks* or *Microsoft Word)*

Newsletter template found in *AppleWorks* or *Microsoft Word* (Optional)

Examples of headlines from real newspapers

PROCEDURE:

1. Divide your class into groups or allow your students to create their own reading groups of four students. Assign or allow the group to choose its own book selection.

2. When each group's selected book is finished, have students brainstorm several possible newspaper headlines from the book. Show students examples of real headlines from local newspapers to assist them with their writing. After the initial brainstorm, have students narrow the list down to four headlines for the newsletter. In the example the following four headlines were chosen from the book:

   • Akiko Arrives on Planet Smoo

   • Rescue Team Captured by Sky Pirates

   • Akiko Defeats the Mighty Jaggasaur with Words!

   • Rescue Team Escapes from Sky Cove

3. Next, have each group create a title for their newsletter.

4. Have each student in the group draft an article for the newsletter using one of the headlines. Have students go through your class's writing process to complete the finished article. If students have little experience with headlines and newspaper-style writing, give minilessons during their writing block.

5. When all articles are completed, have students take turns typing their articles into the same word processing file. Have students select and insert some appropriate clip-art to accompany their article. They can also create their own graphics rather than using clip-art.

6. Have each group appoint one person to "assemble" the newsletter. The "assembler" will need to move the articles into the correct places with their graphics and select an overall style for the newsletter. If students use a template, less assembling will need to be done. (See Figures 4.18 and 4.19.)

7. Have groups print and share their finished newsletters with their classmates.

EXTENSIONS AND ADAPTATIONS:

   • Create a class newsletter for either a read-aloud or a book that each student has to read.

   • Compile a newsletter with articles from several books that students have read.

   • Rather than using just clip-art, require students to use their own graphics or allow them to scan hand-drawn pictures for the newsletter.

   • For younger students whose typing is slow, have a volunteer assemble the articles into a finished newsletter while still allowing the students to have some choice with graphics and style.

Figure 4.18 Page 1 of the newsletter

ADDITIONAL RESOURCES:

Clip-art Resources:

Google Image Surfer: **http://images.google.com**. This section of the Google Search site allows the user to search specifically for images. Type in a search word, and you will be presented with thumbnail images from a variety of Web sites.

ArtToday: **http://www.arttoday.com**. This site charges a fee based on how many weeks you sign up for the service. If you can afford to purchase a year subscription for your classroom, it would be worth the money. If not, consider purchasing a subscription for the length of time students will be working on a project that requires clip-art. The site is easy to navigate, and there is an endless amount of clip-art for almost any topic.

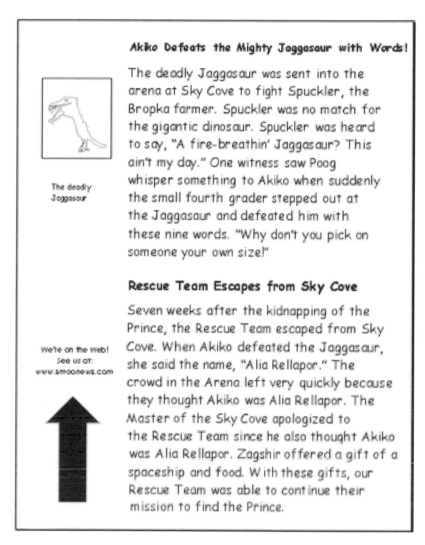

Figure 4.19 Page 2 of the newsletter

Hear, See, and Read

Juster, Norton. *The Phantom Tollbooth*. New York: Random House, Inc., 1961.

OVERVIEW:

As a response to a book students have finished reading, students should select a favorite passage from the book, record themselves reading, and finally, draw an illustration to accompany the words.

GRADE LEVEL:

2–5

MATERIALS:

Multimedia Software *(Hyperstudio, Microsoft Powerpoint,* or *Kid Pix Studio Deluxe)*

PROCEDURE:

1. Using a multimedia program, create a template for students to capture a recording of themselves reading. In your template, there should be a space to enter text as well as a space to add an image (see Figure 4.20).

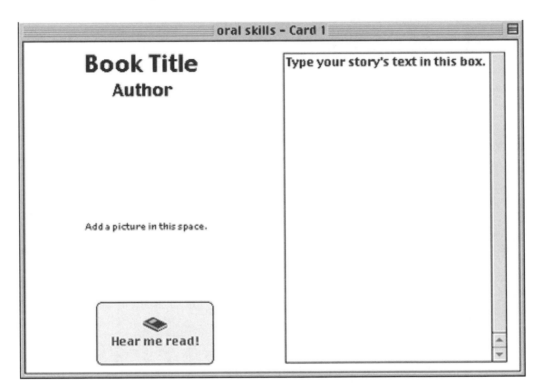

Figure 4.20 Template for capturing reading excerpt
Hyperstudio® and all of its screen images are a registered trademark of Knowledge Adventure, Inc. and are used under license.

2. Have students choose a favorite passage from a book they have recently finished reading. Encourage students to limit the passage to one or two paragraphs if possible. Next, have them type the text into the template on the computer.

3. In the space provided for a graphic, students can scan a picture or draw their own. To record themselves reading, students will need to add a sound. In *Hyperstudio,* they can add a button that plays a sound (see Figure 4.21).

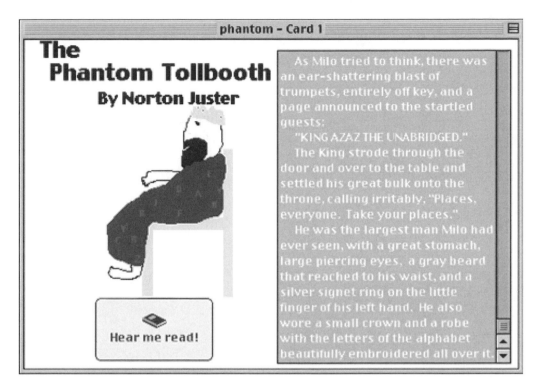

Figure 4.21 Completed card with illustration and excerpt from reading

Hyperstudio® and all of its screen images are a registered trademark of Knowledge Adventure, Inc. and are used under license.

EXTENSIONS AND ADAPTATIONS:

- Use this activity as an assessment tool. Do this at the beginning and end of each school year to show changes in the student's oral reading skills. Choose the same passage to be read aloud and add two buttons to your template. Designate one button for the first reading and the other button for the second reading.

- Extend this multimedia presentation into a larger reading portfolio. Have students create a card for each book they read throughout the school year with an accompanying reflection.

- For younger students, have an older student or parent volunteer assist with the recording and typing. Students can add their own illustration on the card.

- For older students, you may not need to create a template. Allow them to be creative with the design of their card.

ADDITIONAL RESOURCES:

Hyperstudio Walk-through in Appendix A

B's Phantom Tollbooth Page: **http://www.lpl.arizona.edu/~bcohen/phantom-tollbooth/**

Techno Book Reports

Rowling, J.K. *Harry Potter and the Sorcerer's Stone.* New York: Scholastic Inc., 1997.

OVERVIEW:

When a class reads the same book, twenty copies of the same book report can be quite boring for them and for you. Give students an opportunity to share their creativeness and personal strengths by allowing them to choose how they would like to complete their book report with a menu of technological choices.

GRADE LEVEL:

3–5

MATERIALS:

A variety of software choices

Techno Book Reports Reproducible (See Figure 4.23.)

PROCEDURE:

1. Have your students read the same book as part of a genre or thematic unit. (In the example, the teacher's fifth-grade class read *Harry Potter and the Sorcerer's Stone* because although students seemed to talk about the characters and the book a lot, she found that not all had actually read this very famous book.)

2. Before students finish reading the book, explain that they will be completing a technology book report and present the list of choices. Emphasize that we all have different strengths on the computer and encourage students to choose one of the activities that appeals to their strengths.

3. As students finish the book, they can begin working on their projects. With one or two computers in the classroom, you will need to schedule computer time strictly. If your school has a lab, projects can be completed more quickly.

4. Give enough time and support for all students to complete their projects, and when all students are done, provide time for sharing. The projects that will arise from one book will be so diverse (see Figure 4.22).

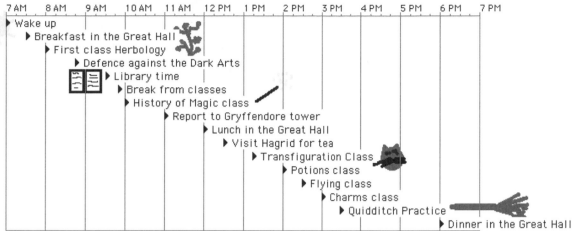

A Day in the Life of Harry Potter

7 AM — 8 AM — 9 AM — 10 AM — 11 AM — 12 PM — 1 PM — 2 PM — 3 PM — 4 PM — 5 PM — 6 PM — 7 PM

▶ Wake up
  ▶ Breakfast in the Great Hall
    ▶ First class Herbology
      ▶ Defence against the Dark Arts
        ▶ Library time
          ▶ Break from classes
            ▶ History of Magic class
              ▶ Report to Gryffendore tower
                ▶ Lunch in the Great Hall
                  ▶ Visit Hagrid for tea
                    ▶ Transfiguration Class
                      ▶ Potions class
                        ▶ Flying class
                          ▶ Charms class
                            ▶ Quidditch Practice
                              ▶ Dinner in the Great Hall

Figure 4.22 Example of student timeline from choice #5

This timeline was created using TimeLiner™ 5.0 by Tom Snyder Productions.

EXTENSIONS AND ADAPTATIONS:

- Offer technology choices year-round but be aware of the student who prefers not to use technology all the time.

- Modify or create your own menu of technological book reports or incorporate the technology choices into students' everyday book report choices.

- For younger students, you may want to introduce them to some of the choices as a class throughout the school year and allow them a choice after they have had considerable exposure to the programs.

ADDITIONAL RESOURCE:

Scholastic's Harry Potter Web site: **http://www.scholastic.com/harrypotter**

Techno

Book

Reports

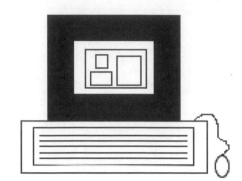

1. Draw your favorite scene from the book in a drawing or painting program. Give your scene a title and include the Chapter title or number.

2. Create a character web in the program Inspiration showing all of the important characters in the book and their personal qualities.

3. Pick your favorite character and illustrate them in a drawing program. Also type some interesting information about them next to the picture.

4. Make a Book Report card in a program where you can create greeting cards. The front should have the title of the book. The inside should have an important character. The other inside panel should have an important setting and the back panel should give a summary of the book.

5. Pretend you are one of the characters for a day. What would a typical day look like. Create a timeline showing your day!

6. Create a Web site for the book. Create a few links to information about the book or author. Share your opinions with other people and include a couple graphics.

7. Write a one page letter to another character in the book or write a diary entry from the perspective of the character. Use a word processing program to complete the letter or diary entry.

8. Create your own project to be approved by your teacher.

Figure 4.23 Techno Book Reports Reproducible

Video Reviews

Cronin, Doreen. *Click, Clack, Moo Cows that Type.* Illustrated by Betsy Lewin. New York: Simon and Schuster, 2000.

OVERVIEW:

Video is technology, and although we often use it with prepared footage, we forget the benefits of creating new learning products. In this activity, students will begin by creating a script for a video, and then using the video camera, they will tape each other reviewing a recent book they have read.

GRADE LEVEL:

K–5

MATERIALS:

Video Camera

Script Reproducible (See Figure 4.24.)

Video-Editing Software (Optional)

PROCEDURE:

1. After reading an independent selection, have students prepare a script of what they will say about their book using the **Script** reproducible. (Students can also use a word processor to type their script.) Any actions or props that will be seen should be described and a visual can be drawn in the box on the left-hand side. The lines are for the students to write what they will say as they are being taped. Students should include a catchy introduction, a short summary, why they liked or disliked the book, and other useful information.

   Sample script:

   Click, Clack, Moo Cows that Type
   Review by Zachary

   Click Clack Moo Cows that Type? I've never heard of cows that can type but these ones do. Farmer Brown has a problem with his typing cows. They want electric blankets. They go on strike when he doesn't bring any. He thinks his cows should do what they are told. Can you believe that? You will have to read more to find out who wins and what the other animals in the barn do. I really like this book. It had a very funny ending and it is funny to imagine cows typing on a typewriter.

2. Have students rehearse their review before they are videotaped.

3. Videotape the book reviews.

4. Share the finished tapes with the rest of the class or store them in the class library so students can preview them when choosing a book to read.

EXTENSIONS AND ADAPTATIONS:

- Have students create a special background for their book review that is specific to their book. You could also create a generic background for use by all students.

- With a small amount of training, older students can videotape each other's performances and then edit their work with a partner.

- Have students use video-editing software to add sound effects, background music, title screens, or credits.

- With younger students, videotape their performances. If you choose to edit the performances using video-editing software, work with students individually or have a parent volunteer assist.

- Have students read a short excerpt from their book as part of their recording.

ADDITIONAL RESOURCES:

Books on Video in the Classroom:

Bazeli, Marilyn J., and James L. Heintz. *Technology across the Curriculum: Activities and Ideas*. Englewood, CO: Libraries Unlimited, 1997.

Fowler, Joel P., and Adrienne L. Herrell. *Camcorder in the Classroom: Using the Video-camera to Enliven Curriculum*. Upper Saddle River, NJ: Prentice Hall, 1997.

Black, K. *Kidvid: Fun-damentals of Video Instruction*. Tucson, AZ: Zephyr Press, 1989.

Web Sites:

Apple iMovie™: **http://www.apple.com/imovie**. This site offers information about Apple's video-editing software.

Apple-Digital Hub for Education: **http://www.apple.com/education/dv/**

Video Planning Sheet

Scene _____

_____
_____
_____
_____
_____

Scene _____

_____
_____
_____
_____
_____

Scene _____

_____
_____
_____
_____
_____

Figure 4.24 Script Reproducible

Other Great Video Ideas

- Video Replay—Replay a favorite scene or alternate ending! Break into groups, and have each group write a script from a scene in the book and act it out on video.

- Reading aloud/Oral reading—Older students can tape themselves reading a book for younger students, or younger students could read a favorite book on tape and watch their favorite story again and again.

- Interview with a character—Have students dress up as their favorite character and prepare a script of questions for themselves. Have another student be the interviewer while another person tapes.

- Talk show format with several characters—Have a small group of students dress up as characters from the same book. Have one student be the talk show host and ask questions about their actions in the book.

- Videotape a book discussion between a small group of students. Later, students can watch their conversation or students who might be interested in the book could listen to the conversation.

- Bring a piece of poetry alive by filming video clips of sights associated with the poem and have the students narrate the video by replacing the sound with a reading of the poem.

CHAPTER 5

Making Use of the Internet

The Internet opens up exciting possibilities with children's literature. Biographical author information abounds on Web sites while original stories are published at an increasing rate. It is your job to sift through all this material to find the best resources for students and to create activities that extend students' comprehension and understanding of literature. Fortunately, though, dedicated librarians and teachers have already done much of the sifting. The activities in this chapter should provide guided experiences to expose students to what is available on the Internet. The last activity in this chapter demonstrates that our eventual goal should be to create students that independently and responsibly search the Internet for the resources they need. Before students go online, discuss online safety and netiquette. In addition, if your school has an Acceptable Use Policy or similar Internet contract be sure that all students have signed and agreed to the rules.

Using Online Literature

Le, Marianne. *Mousie's Adventures.* The Internet Public Library (June 1, 2002): **http://www.ipl.org/div/kidspace/storyhour/**

OVERVIEW:

Online literature occurs in a variety of formats. Some stories can be read as text on Web pages while others are available as downloadable ebooks. The available stories are usually out-of-print books, fairy tales, classics, or original stories by children and adult authors. Although the choices for online literature are still fairly limited, as time passes more and more books are becoming accessible in an electronic format. In this activity, you will demonstrate how to access an online story from a Web page, and students will use the class computer to access an individual selection.

GRADE LEVEL:

K–5

MATERIALS:

Online Story

Overhead Projection Device

PROCEDURE:

1. Find an online short story using the Web sites in the Additional Resources section. In the example, *Mousie's Adventures* was found at The Internet Public Library's Story Hour section (see Figure 5.1).

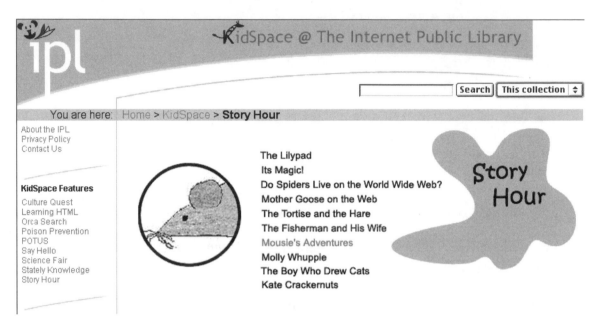

Figure 5.1 The Internet Public Library Story Hour Site

The Internet Public Library © 2002 The Regents of the University of Michigan.

2. Demonstrate how to access the story and show other choices that the Story Hour site offers. Read the selected story together as a class on an overhead projector. In *Mousie's Adventures,* the story can be viewed as text only or with illustrations (see Figure 5.2).

Figure 5.2 Illustrated story page from *Mousie's Adventures*

The Internet Public Library © 2002 The Regents of the University of Michigan.

3. During students' independent reading time, designate a computer as a reading station for students who are between books or would simply like to try one of the Story Hour selections. Load the Web page in advance so students can jump right into reading. Students may also print the text selection if they prefer to read offline.

4. After students finish the selection, have them respond to the reading by opening a drawing program and illustrating a favorite scene from the story (see Figure 5.3).

Figure 5.3 Student's illustrated response to online story
Taken from KidPix® Studio. ©Broderbund Properties LLC. Used with permission.

EXTENSIONS AND ADAPTATIONS:

- Copy and paste the text of a story into an application such as *Simpletext* (available on Macintosh® systems) so students can hear the story read aloud on the computer. This can be especially important for students with special needs. If you are using a Windows® system, use a downloadable utility like *Narrator.* For more information about *Narrator,* go to **http://www.microsoft.com.**

- Copy and paste the text of the story into a word processing program. Use the dictionary feature of your word processor to look up difficult vocabulary words.

- Discuss with your students the experience of reading an online story. Is it easier to read a story on the computer screen or a story in a book? Which do you prefer and why?

- Some authors post excerpts of their newest books online to intrigue readers. Use an excerpt to give students exposure to a new author or to present a book that they might be drawn to read further.

- Bring an old classic to life with modern computer-generated drawings. Copy and paste the text of an online story into a drawing or storybook program and have students add the illustrations.

- Take the previous extension one step further by creating a Web site of the story with the illustrations and text posted online. Have a separate Web page for each section of the story. See "The Many Faces of Alice," a classroom project where students posted the story online with pictures. **http://www.dalton.org/ms/alice**

ADDITIONAL RESOURCES:

Online Book Sites:

Stone Soup: **http://www.stonesoup.com**. This magazine publishes young authors' stories in print and online.

Candlelight Stories: **http://www.candlelightstories.com**

Project Gutenberg: **http://www.gutenberg.net**

StoryBookOnline.Net: **http://www.storybookonline.net/**. This site offers multimedia reading of novels and short stories. This site seeks original submissions and is made up of copyright-free material.

Online Children's Stories: **http://www.acs.ucalgary.ca/~dkbrown/stories.html**. Provides links to multiple story collections.

Internet Public Library's Reading Zone: **http://www.ipl.org/kidspace/browse/rzn0000**

Kid's Corner Featuring Beatrix Potter: **http://www.tcom.ohiou.edu/books/kids.htm**

Storyville on Alfy.com: **http://www.alfy.com/Storyville/**

Tiger the Kitten: **http://www.tigerthekitten.com**

Submit an Online Review

Howe, Deborah and James. *Bunnicula*. Illustrated by Alan Daniel. New York: Scholastic, 1979.

OVERVIEW:

The opinions of other readers help us to decide what we might like to read, and the Internet has become a great resource to find others' opinions. In this activity, students will learn how to access other people's book reviews, write their own, and finally submit their book review online.

GRADE LEVEL:

3–5

MATERIALS:

Web site(s) where students can read and submit online reviews (See Additional Resources section.)

Submitting a Great Online Book Review Reproducible (See Figure 5.4.)

Overhead Projection Device

PROCEDURE:

1. Discuss as a class why it is valuable to read reviews. How do readers choose their books? Read a couple of reviews from a Web site that you have preselected. Discuss what makes an excellent or poor review.

2. Choose a book that students have had a shared experience with such as a recent read-aloud. Show students how you would search for and find the book on a bookstore Web site.

3. Copy and distribute the reproducible, **Submitting a Great Online Book Review** and review how students would fill out the top half of the page using the bookstore Web page.

4. Locate where you submit a review and have students share their thoughts and opinions while you demonstrate how to input a review into the online form.

5. Following the demonstration, have students choose the book they most recently finished for their own review. Have them create a draft using the reproducible. They should also have an editing conference with a peer or you before they submit their final review online.

6. Have students go to the online bookstore Web site. Starting with step two on the reproducible, have students fill in the blanks for the book information. Following the remaining directions, students can enter in the text of their book review. After submitting, students can print the previewed review and post them in the classroom for others to read.

Here is a sample student review that was posted online:

In this book the Monroes go to see a Dracula movie and find a bunny that they bring home. The Monroes also have a dog, Harold and a cat named Chester. Chester is sure that Bunnicula is a vampire bunny because of how he looks and because the vegetables get sucked dry. Chester does some pretty crazy things to try to prove that Bunnicula is a vampire bunny. You'll have to read the book to find out more. I recommend this book to kids who like really funny books and who also like books about spooky things. This book is good for kids from 7–11.

EXTENSIONS AND ADAPTATIONS:

- Design your own guidelines for a book review with your students.

- Bookmark several sites that post book reviews and have students access these reviews to select their next independent reading selection.

- Post student reviews on a school or class Web site so that other schools can check out your students' opinions.

ADDITIONAL RESOURCES:

Web sites with student reviews:

Amazon.com: **http://www.amazon.com**
Barnes and Noble Online Bookstore: **http://www.barnesandnoble.com**
Just for Kids Who Love Books: **http://www3.sympatico.ca/alanbrown/kids.html**
Ann Arbor District Library presents The World of Reading: **http://www.world reading.org/**
Kids Bookshelf Brings Kids and Books Together: **http://www.kidsbookshelf.com/ Book**

Submitting a Great Online Book Review

Name: _____

Book Title: _____

1.) Draft your review before you get online:

Title for Review: _____

Write your review on the back of this page:
(Maximum of 200 words)
Your review should include:
- A summary (Don't give away the ending!)
- What you liked
- What you did not like
- Who would like to read this book
- Any other useful information

**2.) Search for the information below using an online bookstore.
Try this Web site: http://**

Author: _____

Illustrator: _____

Average Customer Rating: _____stars

Your rating: _____stars

People who bought this book also bought:

_____

_____

**3. Submit your review using this Web site.
http://**

4. Check back to see if your review has been posted online.

5. Print it out!

Figure 5.4 Book Review Reproducible

Scavenger Hunts

Cannon, Janell. *Stellaluna*. New York: Harcourt Brace and Company, 1993.

OVERVIEW:

Scavenger hunts provide students with solid facts and information on a topic. They consist of questions followed by Internet links where students can find the answers. You have the task of finding links that hold relevant and essential knowledge for your learners and then pairing up the links to important questions. With this book-centered scavenger hunt, students will learn more about bats and the book *Stellaluna.*

GRADE LEVEL:

2–5

MATERIALS:

Scavenger Hunt Reproducible(s) (See Figures 5.5 and 5.6.)

PROCEDURE:

1. Read *Stellaluna* aloud to your students.

2. Develop a scavenger hunt for your students by searching for Internet sites that center around the book's theme and/or author.

3. Next, develop questions that can be answered from the Web sites that you have found (see Figure 5.7).

4. Complete the **Scavenger Hunt** reproducible that best fits your topic and the students' grade level. If you are working with students who have little experience with the Internet, use the first reproducible (Figure 5.6). With this layout, students will know which link directly corresponds to which question. For older more experienced students, you may want to use the second reproducible (Figure 5.7). The answers will be harder to find because students will not know which link provides the answer to the question.

5. Reproduce and distribute the scavenger hunt to students. Give students time online to find the answers.

6. After completing the scavenger hunt, discuss what students learned from the Web sites. Were there any Web sites they would like to revisit? Do they know of any other Web sites where information could be found about bats or the book?

EXTENSIONS AND ADAPTATIONS:

- Create your scavenger hunt online using a Web page tool like *Filamentality*. Posting the hunt online allows your students to click directly on the links instead of typing in each Web address. **http://www.filamentality.com/wired/fil/**

- Bookmark the sites you wish students to use in the scavenger hunt so they are easily accessible.

- Search for scavenger hunts that have already been posted online by other teachers.

ADDITIONAL RESOURCES:

Trackstar: **http://trackstar.hprtec.org/**. This site allows a teacher to create a list of Web sites that may be useful for a particular lesson, research, or a scavenger hunt.

Stellaluna CD published by The Learning Company

Title:_____

Name:_____

Introduction:

▶ Link 1:

? Question(s):

▶ Link 2:
? Question(s):

▶ Link 3:
? Question(s):

? Final Question:

Figure 5.5 Scavenger Hunt Reproducible

Title:_____

Name:_____

Introduction:

? Questions:

▶ Links:

? Final Question:

Figure 5.6 Scavenger Hunt Reproducible

Stellaluna Scavenger Hunt

Name:_____

Below is a list of questions about bats and the book Stellaluna. Surf the Internet sites on this page to find the answers to the questions. Have fun!

▶ Link 1: Bats: A Thematic Resource for Teachers and Students
http://intergate.cccoe.k12.ca.us/bats/

? Question(s):

Take the bat quiz. What was your score?____

Go to the science section and check out the anatomy of a bat. List three things that bats and people have in common.
1.
2.
3.

▶ Link 2: Bats, Bats, Everywhere! http://members.aol.com/bats4kids/
? Question(s):
List three places where bats might live?

What kind of foods do bats eat?

Are bats a mammal or a bird? Why?

▶ Link 3: Barnes and Noble Bookstore
http://www.barnesandnoble.com
? Question(s):
Search for Janell Cannon at the book store. List two other books that she has written.
1.
2.

What do you think the author likes to write about?

? Final Question:
Find your favorite kind of bat using one of the sites above. List one interesting fact about this bat.

Figure 5.7 *Stellaluna* **Scavenger Hunt**

Book Chats

Creech, Sharon. *Love that Dog.* New York: HarperCollins Publishers, 2001.

OVERVIEW:

When we dialogue about books with our students, we broaden our understanding of the text and develop new insights. Because assorted readers from various backgrounds come to the discussion, new perspectives and differing opinions can be heard. An online dialogue can further students' understanding with an entirely new point of view. Instead of the typical gatherings with a teacher or fellow classmates, the experience is extended to a class down the hall or a class from another country. This activity describes how to plan for and conduct a book discussion over the Internet. Make sure your students have participated in book discussions with peers in their own class and are fairly confident with the process before they embark on an Internet discussion.

GRADE LEVEL:

3–5

MATERIALS:

Chat Room or Discussion Location

Brainstorming Reproducible (See Figure 5.10.)

PROCEDURE:

1. Create a chat room for students to conduct their discussion within. Use a site like ePALS Classroom Exchange™ **(http://www.epals.com)**. To create a chat room with ePALSTM, click on "Join ePALS" to register for a new account. Once registered, you can create a private chat room using the Communication Tools.

2. Contact a teacher who is interested in discussing a book via chat. Mutually decide on a book for your classes to discuss. It is best to start small, so try your first chat with another class in the same school. If you wish to work with a class from another state or country, use a mailing list or Web site that assists in matching classes.

3. When your students have finished reading the book, decide on a time and day to meet the other class in your private chat room. Give the participating teacher the chat room's URL, chat room name, and the chat room password so they can login (see Figure 5.8). Be sure to also discuss the protocol your classes will follow when in the chat room. For example, one class submits a question or answer and the other class responds with a question or answer.

Figure 5.8 Example of chat room login

4. Before the date of the scheduled discussion, show your students the location of the chat room. Login and allow students to write comments back and forth to familiarize themselves with the process. Be sure to discuss online etiquette and safety. Do not give the password to students because they would be able to logon from home, and you would be unable to monitor any conversation.

5. Reproduce and distribute the **Brainstorming** reproducible. To prepare for the live chat, have students record both comments and questions about the book.

6. At the designated time and place, load the chat room site on a computer connected to an overhead projector. Have students take turns coming up to the screen to ask questions and offer thoughts while you read aloud the back-and-forth conversation (see Figure 5.9).

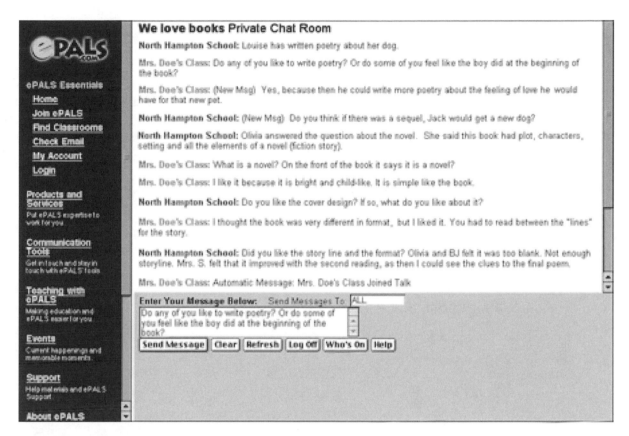

Figure 5.9 Chat room conversation between two classes

EXTENSIONS AND ADAPTATIONS:

- Prepare students for in-depth conversations by starting with e-mail exchanges or limit the conversations to two or three questions that you and the participating teacher have decided on ahead of time.

- Discuss other literature topics in a chat room such as favorite fantasy books or favorite characters.

- Use a discussion board instead of a chat room. In a discussion board, a participant submits a question or thought, and others can comment at any time. In a chat room, you see the comments as they are typed similar to a phone conversation.

- If you want to begin on an even smaller scale, choose a group of three to four students who are reading the same book and match them to another group in the classroom.

ADDITIONAL RESOURCES:

Web sites:

ePALS Classroom Exchange™: **http://www.epals.com**. Find connections to students and classes from all over the world. The site allows you to create a password-protected chat room. There is also an On-line Book Club.

The Read In!: **http://www.readin.org.** This is an annual event where students from around the world come together to talk to authors about their books. Check the Web site for information on how to join the event and which authors will be appearing.

Scholastic: **http://www.scholastic.com**. This site offers discussion questions on favorite books and occasional live author chats.

KidLink: **http://www.kidlink.org**. Go to this site to learn how to join their mailing list.

Classroom Connect's Author Chats: **http://www.authorchats.com/lit/**

Sharon Creech's Web site: **http://www.sharoncreech.com**

For more information on Literature Circles:

Eeds, Maryann, and Ralph Peterson. *Grand Conversations*. New York: Scholastic Inc., 1990.

Daniels, Harvey. *Literature Circles: Voice and Choice in Book Clubs and Reading Groups*. York, ME: Stenhouse Publishers, 2001.

Book Brainstorming

Title:_____ Author:_____

Thoughts	Questions

Figure 5.10 Brainstorming Reproducible

Using Author Web Pages

Pilkey, Dav. *'Twas the Night before Thanksgiving*. New York: Scholastic, 1990.

OVERVIEW:

More often, authors are making their presence known on the Internet. Many well-known authors have their own home pages with biographical information and activities for their fans. Even if an author does not have a home page, a wealth of information exists on other sites on the Internet. Using the Web to supplement a book or author study is valuable because the medium is engaging and the information is up to date. After students are introduced to an author through a read-aloud, students will use the author's Web site to choose their next independent reading selection.

GRADE LEVEL:

2–5

MATERIALS:

Author Web site (http://www.pilkey.com)

Overhead Projection Device

PROCEDURE:

1. Find an author Web site such as *Author and Illustrator Dav Pilkey's Web Site O' Fun* that is related to an author study you are conducting or to a book your class is reading. Review and bookmark the site (see Figure 5.11).

2. With your class, load the site on a computer connected to an overhead projection device and explore the site. Call attention to the Table of Contents and how the site is organized.

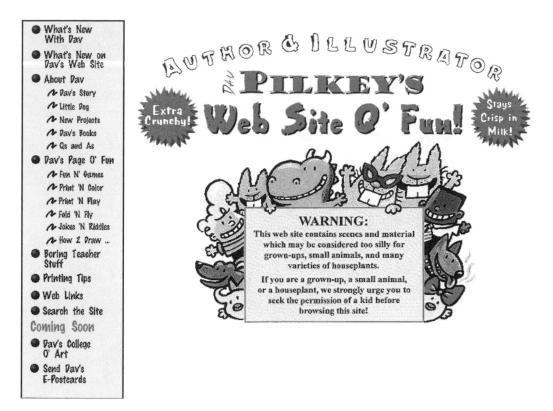

Figure 5.11

From AUTHOR AND ILLUSTRATOR DAV PILKEY'S WEBSITE O'FUN. Copyright © 1997 by Dav Pilkey. Reprinted by permission of Writers House, LLC.

3. Click on the link titled "Dav's Books." A list of books will appear on the next page. Select the one you read aloud to your class. Read the summary of the book and take the quiz at the bottom of the page with your class (see Figure 5.12).

About Dav

| Dav's Story | Dav's Books | Little Dog | Dav's New Projects | Qs and As |

CLICK HERE FOR CURRENT PRICES AT AMAZON.COM

'Twas the Night Before Thanksgiving

CLICK HERE FOR Reviews!

Publisher: Orchard Books **ISBN:** 0-933849-22-2

What it's About:

It's Autumn, and a classroom of children are on their way to a field trip at Mack Nugget's turkey farm. The children and the turkeys become best of pals, but their bliss ends when the children discover what's in store for their fine feathered friends. Can the children save the turkeys from certain doom? Find out in this silly and warm-hearted parody of Clement Moore's classic tale, *'Twas the Night Before Christmas*.

'Twas the Night Before Thanksgiving has become one of the most popular Thanksgiving books of all time. But believe it or not, this book was rejected 23 times by 23 different publishers. Dav was so discouraged by all the rejections, he *almost* quit writing children's books altogether. Finally, Orchard Books accepted the book, though they didn't expect it to sell many copies. As it turned out, the book that nobody wanted to publish ended up surprising everyone. *'Twas the Night Before Thanksgiving* has become the third largest selling picturebook in Orchard Books' history.

Dav Pilkey wrote *'Twas the Night Before Thanksgiving* because a librarian in Cleveland told him to write a Thanksgiving book. Never one to question a librarian, Dav began working on this book right away. He went out to the middle of a cow pasture with a large quilt and a tablet of yellow

Figure 5.12

From AUTHOR AND ILLUSTRATOR DAV PILKEY'S WEBSITE O'FUN. Copyright © 1997 by Dav Pilkey. Reprinted by permission of Writers House, LLC.

4. Explain to students that they will be selecting the next book they read from Dav's list of books. Give them time to explore the titles and read some of the summaries. Ask students to create a list of three books they would be interested in reading. Students should then choose one book to read and locate it in the school or classroom library.

5. When students have finished the book, have them go back to the Web site and take the quiz on their specific book.

EXTENSIONS AND ADAPTATIONS:

*   If the author has an e-mail address have your students generate a list of questions to send. (Some authors welcome e-mail correspondence whereas others do not.) Before students construct questions, they should read any interviews or biographical information from books or Web sites. By researching the author prior to planning an e-mail conversation, you will immediately know which questions not to ask. You can also use e-mail as a means to prepare for an upcoming author's visit or if your school cannot afford to bring an author to visit, substitute a visit with e-mail conversations.

- Develop an extensive author scavenger hunt where all of the answers can be located on the author's Web site.

- Use the Web site's teacher resources to plan lessons. Many authors offer book summaries, fun worksheets, and suggestions for using their Web site.

ADDITIONAL RESOURCES:

Great Author Web sites:

Jan Brett's Homepage: **http://www.janbrett.com**
Eric Carle's Official Web site: **http://www.eric-carle.com**
David Wiesner: **http://www.houghtonmifflinbooks.com/authors/wiesner/home.html**
Just for Kids Who Love Books: **http://www3.sympatico.ca/alanbrown/kids.html**.
   Provides links to author pages and e-mail addresses.
Yahooligans Children's Author Index: **http://www.yahooligans.com/school_bell/ language_arts/Authors/**
Yahooligans Illustrators Index: **http://www.yahooligans.com/School_Bell/Language_ Arts/Illustrators/**

Scholastic Author Studies:

   http://www2.scholastic.com/teachers/authorsandbooks/authorstudies/author studies.jhtml

Celebrate a Book with a Web Page

Cherry, Lynne. *The Armadillo from Amarillo.* San Diego: Harcourt Brace and Company, 1994.

OVERVIEW:

   The Internet is often used for finding more information on a topic, but it is also a place to publish information and projects for others to learn from. In this project, students are enlisted to create a class Web page that celebrates a book. Students are given the chance to design the pages, to publish their findings, and to provide a valuable reading resource for other classrooms.

GRADE LEVEL:

   K–5

MATERIALS:

   Software to create Web sites or a Web site that allows you to create your own Web site easily. (Creating a Web page can be a very involved process or can be quite simple. This all depends on how you decide to create the page. See the Additional Resources section.)

   Word Processing Software

   Graphics Software

PROCEDURE:

1. Discuss with your class the Web page they will be creating. Explain that the Web page will be about the book they have recently read or one that you have read to them. The Internet is a place to find information and also a place to publish information for others. Ask your students what would they like to share with other classes from around the world? Brainstorm what types of information your students would like to include on their Web site. Following is the brainstorm from a third-grade class using the example *The Armadillo from Amarillo* by Lynne Cherry:

Information about maps

Information about armadillos

Information about eagles

A map of the armadillo's route

A map of Texas

A map of the United States

A map of the world

Information about the Space Program

Information about the Space Shuttle

Information about the moon

Information about the planets

Description of where we live! Where in the world are we? Could other students e-mail us to let us know where they live?

Postcard for kids to send to each other

Is there really an armadillo at the Philadelphia Zoo?

Information about the different habitats (prairie, woodland, plains)

Information about animals in Texas

More books by Lynne Cherry

Information on why or how she made this book

2. Decide which ideas are feasible and focus the Web page by having the class narrow the list down to four or five items. In the example, some ideas were chosen and other ideas were consolidated into one.

    Here were the final four items that were chosen by the third-grade class.

    1. Where are we in the world? Other classes could e-mail us so we could post their responses too.

2. Information about armadillos and other Texas animals

3. Maps of the locations in the book (Texas, United States, world, moon, planets)

4. Information about Lynne Cherry, her books, and why she wrote this book.

3. Divide your class into groups to complete the necessary work. If students will be creating the actual Web page files, then you will probably need to teach them how to use the program of choice.

Here are the four group tasks:

Group 1 Where are we in the world?—This will be the title page. Work on a description on where we are. Type it into the computer and find or create any graphics for the page.

Group 2 Texas Animals—This will be a page that links off the home page. Do research and write small reports on different Texas animals that appeared in the book. Find good Internet links for other students to use.

Group 3 Maps of places in the book—This will be a page that links off the home page. Gather images or Web sites that display the locations in the book. Students may make their own map of Texas showing the Armadillo's land route.

Group 4 Information about Lynne Cherry and her books—This will be a page that links off the home page. Gather a list of books by Lynne Cherry. Find information about the author and the book, *The Armadillo from Amarillo*.

4. Allow time for your students to complete the necessary work. When finished, collect your students' work including all word processing files and graphics. Depending on how your site was created, you can allow students to make the Web pages or you can take their files and use them to make the pages on your own.

5. Have a class party when you upload the finished page(s). Give students the Web site address and distribute it to community and parents (see Figure 5.13).

Where are we in the World?

Our teacher read us the book, The Armadillo from Amarillo by Lynne Cherry. After we read the book we decided to make a Web page. This is our Web page about the book and it's author. Click on the links below to go to our other pages.

We are in the Town of Gardiner
In the Great State of Maine
In the Country of the United States
In the Continent of North America
On the Planet Earth

E-mail us!
Let us know where you are and we will post it on our site.

Maps

Animals

More about Lynne Cherry and her books

Last updated on 3/23/02

Figure 5.13 Home page demonstrating the work by Group 1

EXTENSIONS AND ADAPTATIONS:

- Use *Inspiration* to create a diagram of how the Web site will be organized (see Figure 5.14). This will give students a more concrete understanding of what the final product will look like.

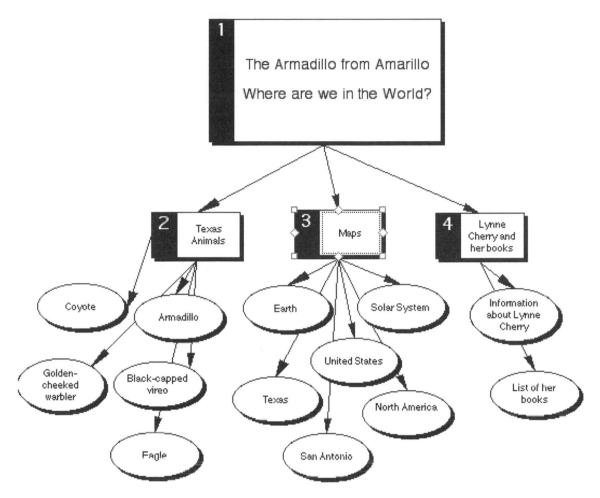

Figure 5.14 Web site diagram
This diagram was created using Inspiration® by Inspiration Software®, Inc.

- For younger classes, decide ahead of time the content for the Web page.

- Many things can be published on a classroom Web site. Use the site to post book projects, student book reviews, or pictures of your students during reading time.

ADDITIONAL RESOURCES:

Software:

Microsoft Word or *AppleWorks.* With these word processing programs you can save your word files as Web page files. Then the files just need to be uploaded to an available server.

Site Central™ published by Knowledge Adventure®

Web sites for creating a Web page easily:

Teacher Web: **http://www.teacherweb.com**
Scholastic Web site: **http://teacher.scholastic.com/homepagebuilder/index.htm**
PLACEMARK™: **http://www.placemark.tomsnyder.com/placemark**. Easy way to manage and create a class site.

Using the Internet for Authentic Research

Kerley, Barbara. *The Dinosaurs of Waterhouse Hawkins.* Illustrated by Brian Selznick. New York: Scholastic Inc., 2001

OVERVIEW:

Students' first experiences with the Internet should be carefully guided. Eventually, though, students need to be able to identify which sites are valid and from reputable sources. As teachers, we can be there to help evaluate the accurateness of the sites they find and also teach them to conduct better searches. In this activity, students are allowed to search freely for information on a story and related theme. This experience is both highly motivating and exciting as each student discovers more about the topic through the text, images, and sounds of the Internet.

GRADE LEVEL:

4–5

MATERIALS:

Keywords Reproducible (See Figure 5.15.)

Overhead Projection Device

PROCEDURE:

1. Begin by reading aloud the book to your students. Choose a book with historical significance, such as *The Dinosaurs of Waterhouse Hawkins.* In the back of the book, there are author and illustrator notes that describe in detail some of the historical events and key people.

2. Reproduce and distribute the **Keywords** reproducible. As a class, generate a list of keywords from the book. Think back to people, places, and things that were important to the story and fill in the words into the appropriate columns. Encourage students to add additional keywords to their lists.

   Sample Keywords:

   Benjamin Waterhouse Hawkins

   Queen Victoria

   Richard Owen

The Crystal Palace

The Paleozoic Museum

Boss Tweed

Sydenham Park

Iguanodon

Central Park

Barbara Kerley

Megalosaurus

3. Bring students to a lab setting if it is available. If not, create a schedule for students to complete the task on one or two available computers. Tell students that they are about to find as much information on the dinosaurs of Waterhouse Hawkins and the book by Barbara Kerley using the Internet.

4. Use a popular search engine and one of the keywords from the class brainstorm to demonstrate how you would conduct a search for relevant Web sites. Choose one related site and pick out important or interesting information. (If students need some suggestions for search engines, post a list in the classroom.)

5. Open a word processor and show students how you would input notes from the information discovered. Ask them to record the Web addresses of some of the sites they think are the best. Give students the option of taking notes using either their word processor or pencil and paper.

6. As students search and take notes, encourage them to share their findings with you. The excitement can be contagious!

7. At the end of the searching session, leave time for students to share their exciting discoveries with the entire class.

What one fourth-grade class discovered:

- I found a real picture of one of Waterhouse Hawkins's models.

- I found a picture of Brian Selznick sitting under a model of a dinosaur in Sydenham Park. This must have been his trip to London to draw the dinosaurs.

- I found a page about a guy named Gideon Mantell. He supposedly decided that the big spiked tooth that belonged to the Iguanadon was a spike on his nose. I thought in the book that Waterhouse Hawkins decided that the spike belonged on the nose, but maybe not?

- I found a picture of Benjamin Waterhouse Hawkins sitting in a chair.

- I found a picture that Waterhouse Hawkins drew of the dinosaurs at Sydenham Park.

- I found a Web page with information on the Paleozoic Museum that was supposed to be built in Central Park. The book said it was going to look like the Crystal Palace, but this Web page said that it was going to be just columns that held up a roof. One dinosaur was going to be attacking another. An artist drew a picture of what they thought it would look like and turned it into a Cyclorama. In the 1800s, they would make a really big picture and wrap it around a round room to look like 3-D. On the Web site it was more like virtual reality. It was cool!

- I discovered that there were lots of other scientists that came before and after Hawkins. Hawkins was more like an artist than a scientist and Owens was the guy who helped him to figure out how to draw the dinosaurs.

EXTENSIONS AND ADAPTATIONS:

- If taking notes while searching is too much for your students, allow them to print a couple pages of the most interesting items they find. Make sure you preview what they wish to print. Take the printed pages and collect them into a classroom notebook for students to peruse through for more information.

- Have each student print or download one image from a Web site and create a class collage.

- If you are still concerned about giving your students access to the Internet, limit the search engines that they can use to child-appropriate ones. You could also check with your technology specialist to see if your school has an Internet filter in place.

- The last page of the book illustrates a few of the dinosaurs as they were depicted by Waterhouse Hawkins and how they are believed to look now. Have your students do specific searches for the dinosaurs depicted using the Internet and with *Inspiration* or other concept-mapping software, then compare and contrast the depictions.

ADDITIONAL RESOURCES:

Search Engines:

Google: **http://www.google.com**
Yahooligans: **http://www.yahooligans.com**

Keywords

People	Places	Things

Figure 5.15 Keywords Reproducible

CHAPTER 6

An Introduction to Electronic Books

What is a book? Because of today's technology, a book can be enjoyed in both paper and electronic form. So, if you were presented with a choice of paper or computer screen, what would you choose? It might depend on the book, the content, and even your curriculum.

Electronic books come in a variety of formats. Software publishers have made books available on CD-ROM. A child can read aloud the majority of the CD-ROM books, or a child can choose to "play" with the text and pictures. Some CDs provide additional content in the form of skill-building games or theme-specific information. An ebook is different from a book on CD because it stays truer to the original format of the book (i.e., no animations, games, etc.). An ebook provides benefits to the user from the added features of an integrated dictionary and other note-taking tools. Ebooks are available to download from online bookstores and other free Web sites. They exist in a variety of file formats and can be opened and read by several different software packages. The simplest of ebooks are HTML files (Web pages) that can be read by an Internet browsing program while online or after downloading. Other file formats require more specific ebook reader programs where the reader can experience the ebook similar to a paper format. Pages can be turned with a click of the mouse, electronic notes added in the margins, and important sections of text highlighted.

Electronic books are an ever-evolving technology. More and more books will become available in electronic format, and by the time our students reach college, all their textbooks may be on a handheld computer, whereas CD-ROM books are a dwindling technology and will be increasingly more difficult to find. This chapter demonstrates the basics of electronic text and shows how to introduce students to CD-ROM books, ebooks, and even audio books on the computer. It also illustrates how books in electronic form can be used to engage students in literature and to reinforce literacy skills.

BENEFITS OF ELECTRONIC BOOKS

- Ebooks are convenient to carry from one location to another. Instead of carrying five books in a backpack, all five and probably more can be carried on a laptop or handheld computer.

- Ebooks are environmentally friendly.

- Special Education students with learning or physical disabilities may benefit from the ability to increase the size of the text on the screen or hear the story read aloud.

- An illustrated ebook or CD-ROM book can be projected onto an overhead screen or television to enlarge the pages for better viewing and present the book to larger audiences.

- Because paper is not needed, the cost of electronic books is sometimes much less.

- Our students are growing up in a technological world where they are used to reading text on a computer screen. Therefore, reading an ebook or CD-ROM book should appeal to their familiarity with the multimedia format.

- Click on an unfamiliar word and a CD-ROM book will read it aloud. Highlight it in an ebook and the dictionary feature will supply you with a definition.

- Add notes to the side of the page when you have a question or when you make a connection to the literature.

- Students gain valuable computer skills as they are reading.

- Use the Bookmark or Find feature to locate a particular passage.

- Motivate students to read with a new technology. Students are active participants with interactive text.

Read and Interact with a CD-ROM Book

Seuss, Dr. *Green Eggs and Ham.* New York: Beginner Books, 1960.

OVERVIEW:

Traditionally, students have used books on CD and other educational software during free time or as an incentive. Instead of offering students CD-ROM books as a special reward, teach them how to enjoy and interact with the pictures and text of a CD-ROM book as they would with any book during their reading time. When students interact with the book in a variety of ways, their vocabulary and decoding skills grow stronger. In this activity, students will hear the story read aloud by their teacher, then listen to the computer read the book and spend some time playing . . . I mean learning!

GRADE LEVEL:

K–3

MATERIALS:

Story on CD

Overhead Projection Device

Rules for Computer Reading Reproducible (See Figure 6.3.)

PROCEDURE:

1. Read the book *Green Eggs and Ham* by Dr. Seuss to your students. Students should experience and appreciate a book in its original format before reading and playing with it in a multimedia format.

2. After reading the book, introduce The Learning Company's Living Book *Green Eggs and Ham* by Dr. Seuss™ using an overhead projection device. Point out the two choices students are presented with when they open the program: To read or to play (see Figures 6.1 and 6.2). Demonstrate how the program works in both modes.

Figure 6.1 Starting screen where a student can decide whether to hear the story read aloud or choose to play with the pages

Would you eat
them in a box?
Would you eat
them with a fox?

Not in a 📚.
Not with a 🐱.
Not in a 🏠.
Not with a 🐭.

I would not eat them
👉 or 👉.
I would not eat them
anywhere.

Figure 6.2 Sample page from the *Green Eggs and Ham* CD

3. Review the **Rules for Reading** reproducible with your students. If you wish, copy and distribute the rules to each student.

Teacher Rationale for the Rules for Computer Reading:

1. Find a partner.—Working with a partner allows students to share the funny or sad moments of a story. It will also decrease the computer questions that you as the teacher may receive.

2. Read the book first.—Just as it is important to enjoy a book in its original paper format, it is also important for students to hear the book read on the computer before they can play with it.

3. Choose a favorite page to play and read.—Playing should build and enhance the previous reading experience. Try some of the activities in the Extension and Adaptations section to make the "play time" more valuable.

4. Take turns with the mouse. Five clicks for you, five clicks for me.—Working with a partner at the computer can be difficult for students because they want to control the mouse. To help students monitor their time and play fairly, limit the clicks on each page to five per student.

5. Click on at least one new word.—Students should experiment with the text of the story. Listening to a word read aloud reinforces reading skills.

6. Enjoy.

4. Create a computer station for students to visit so they can read the book with a partner. Post the rules for reading above or nearby the computer.

(To further monitor student's progress, refer to the Extensions and Adaptations section at the end of this activity.)

EXTENSIONS AND ADAPTATIONS:

- If you wish students to have multiple experiences with the text, read the CD-ROM book as a class before students use the book with a partner.

- After students read the book on the computer, have them return to the paper version of the book. After prior experiences of hearing, seeing, and reading the text, students will be able to try out their new vocabulary and decoding skills.

- To evaluate students' reading improvements, complete a running record with the first reading of the book or of a section of the book. After students have worked with the CD-ROM version, complete another running record for comparison.

- To reinforce literacy skills, ask students to point to a word and predict what that word is when read aloud. Then they can click on it to hear its pronunciation.

- To monitor students time in play mode, ask them to predict what an object might do or what a character might say before they click on it. Use the **Predict and Click** reproducible (see Figure 6.4). This activity is appropriate for students who can read and write without support.

- Have students complete a reflection based on their technology-enriched reading experience (see Figure 6.5). With younger students, ask them to share what they liked and disliked with the rest of the class. Use the questions on the reproducible as a guide for students sharing.

ADDITIONAL RESOURCES:

Point, Click, and Predict Reproducible

Reflection Reproducible

Rules for Computer Reading

- Find a partner

- Read the book first.

- Choose a favorite page
  to play and read.

- Take turns with the mouse.
  5 clicks for you. 5 clicks for me.

- Click on at least one new word.

- Enjoy

Figure 6.3 Rules for Computer Reading Reproducible

Predict and Click

Title: _____

I clicked on:	I think it will:	This is what it did:

Figure 6.4 Point, Click, and Predict Reproducible

Computer Reading Reflection

Name:_____

Title:_____

What I liked:

What I did not like:

Do you like reading a book on CD? Why or Why not?

If a software company said they would make a CD-ROM book especially for you, which book would you choose?

Why is this book a good choice?

Figure 6.5 Reflection Reproducible

Creating an Interactive Poetry Book

Prelutsky, Jack. *Something Big Has Been Here.* Illustrated by James Stevenson. New York: William Morrow and Company, Inc., 1990.

OVERVIEW:

After students have had experience reading interactive books on CD, they can better understand the original elements of these electronic versions and create their own. Using multimedia software, students will give sound and movement to words and objects and create a page to showcase their favorite poem.

GRADE LEVEL:

3–5

MATERIALS:

Jack Prelutsky's *The New Kid on the Block* and other examples of stories on CD

Overhead Projection Device

Hyperstudio or Other Multimedia Software

Inspiration Software (Optional)

Multimedia Planning Sheet Reproducible in Appendix B

PROCEDURE:

1. Introduce the activity to students by sharing a CD-ROM book. I recommend showing Jack Prelutsky's *The New Kid on the Block* because it is an example of an interactive poetry book, but any book on CD will do.

2. Brainstorm with students the attributes of CD-ROM books. Use chart paper or *Inspiration* to record the brainstorming session (see Figure 6.6).

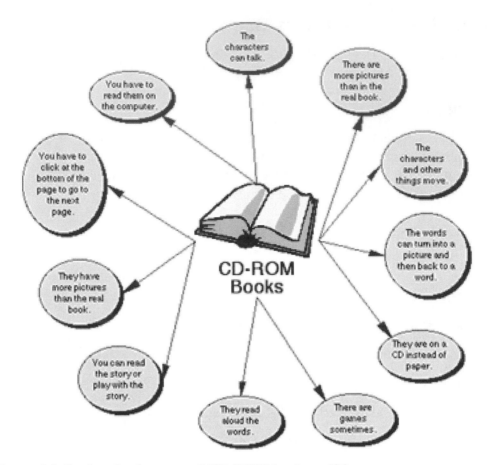

The characters can talk.

There are more pictures than in the real book.

You have to read them on the computer.

The characters and other things move.

You have to click at the bottom of the page to go to the next page.

The words can turn into a picture and then back to a word.

CD-ROM Books

They have more pictures than the real book.

They are on a CD instead of paper.

You can read the story or play with the story.

They read aloud the words.

There are games sometimes.

Figure 6.6 Student brainstorm of CD-ROM book qualities

This diagram was created using Inspiration® by Inspiration Software®, Inc.

3. Explain to students that they will be designing one page similar to the book pages on the CD using a multimedia program like *Hyperstudio.* Have students choose a favorite poem for their interactive book page.

4. Have students plan their cards using the **Multimedia Planning Sheet** reproducible. The planning sheet should have the poem and an illustration. In the Notes section of the planning sheet, students should detail which words and objects will make sounds or be animated.

5. Using the computer, have students create their card (see Figure 6.7). Demonstrate how to make invisible buttons to have words read aloud or to activate sounds and animations.

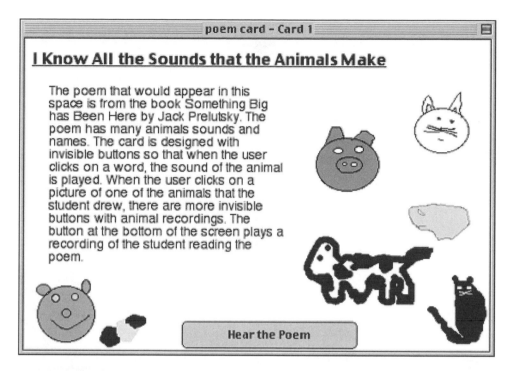

Figure 6.7 Example of student interactive poetry card
Hyperstudio® and all of its screen images are a registered trademark of Knowledge Adventure, Inc. and are used under license.

6. Allow students time to listen to the poems and play with the interactive elements.

EXTENSIONS AND ADAPTATIONS:

- As a supplement to a favorite book, have students create a one-page interactive excerpt.

- Have students create an entire interactive book if time allows.

- For younger students, create a template for them to fill in (see Figure 6.8). Leave one side of the page for an illustration and create a text box on the opposite side where students can type in the text.

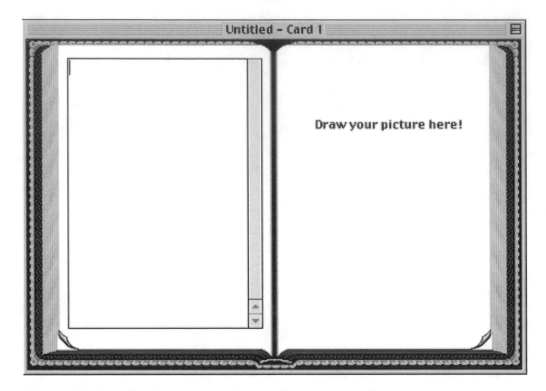

Figure 6.8 Template for creating interactive poetry card
Hyperstudio® and all of its screen images are a registered trademark of Knowledge Adventure, Inc. and are used under license.

- Burn the multimedia "book" to a CD using a CD Burner. Include *Hyperstudio Player* (a program that plays stacks but can not create new ones) and the *Hyperstudio* stack along with any multimedia files that were used to create the stack. Students can take the CD home to try.

- Have your students share their interactive books with younger students.

- Divide a book's pages among students in the class and have each student complete one page.

- Have students choose a piece of their own writing for a book idea.

ADDITIONAL RESOURCES:

Hyperstudio Walk-through in Appendix A
Hyperstudio Player Download from **http://www.hyperstudio.com**

Using Illustrated Ebooks as Read-Alouds

Hansen, T. Cory. *The Last Little Pumpkin.* Illustrated by Carol Foldvary-Anderson. Reno, NV: JetKor, 2001.

OVERVIEW:

Begin teaching students to read an ebook by learning the basics of the software. At the same time provide a learning experience with vocabulary by asking students to search for specific words as you read aloud the book.

GRADE LEVEL:

K–3

MATERIALS:

Adobe® Acrobat® eBook Reader™ or other Ebook Reader Software installed on your computer

Downloaded Story from Online Bookstore or from any free Web site

Overhead Projection Device

PROCEDURE:

1. Choose an electronic picture book to read aloud to your students.

2. Open the book in *Adobe eBook Reader* or another program and using an overhead projection device, show your students the basics of opening a book, turning pages, and accessing the dictionary (see Figure 6.9).

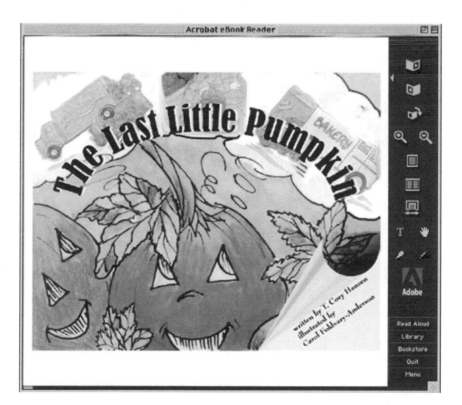

Figure 6.9 Cover page of the illustrated ebook *The Last Little Pumpkin*
Author T. Cory Hansen, Illustrator Carol Foldvary-Anderson, Published by JetKor, Reno, Nevada © 2001.

3. Ask students to look for five key vocabulary words in the story. List the five vocabulary words on chart paper or the chalkboard. When they see one of the five words in the book, they should signal by raising their hands. The following five words were chosen from *The Last Little Pumpkin:*

Nipped

Anticipation

Massive

Blossomed

Visible

4. Read the book to students. As you encounter each new word, highlight the word using the Highlighter tool and then look for the definition using the dictionary feature (see Figure 6.10). (In some picture ebooks the user is unable to highlight words because they are embedded in the page. If this is the case, students could make a note next to the word with a definition.)

5. Create a computer center where students can visit the classroom computer and read the ebook by themselves.

EXTENSIONS AND ADAPTATIONS:

- Before you read, turn to the cover page and ask students to make predictions about the book by looking at the cover and the title. Record their predictions using the Annotation tool. After reading, return to the predictions and see how accurate they were.

- Do two readings of the picture ebook. During the first read, ask students to just listen. During the second read, allow students to share their reactions to the story, ask questions, and connect to the text. Add your own responses as you reread. Add all comments to the ebook with the Annotation tool. See Chapter 7, Comprehension Strategies, for more activities like this.

- With some picture ebooks, the program allows you to hear the text read aloud. Use this feature for emergent or nonreaders.

- Use an ebook to assist in teaching a guided reading lesson with a small group of students. Print out multiple copies of the book for students and use the electronic version for teacher demonstration.

- Discuss with your students the experience of reading an ebook. Is it easier to read a story on the computer screen or in a book? Which do you prefer and why?

- Using the Zoom In feature, make the text larger for students with special needs.

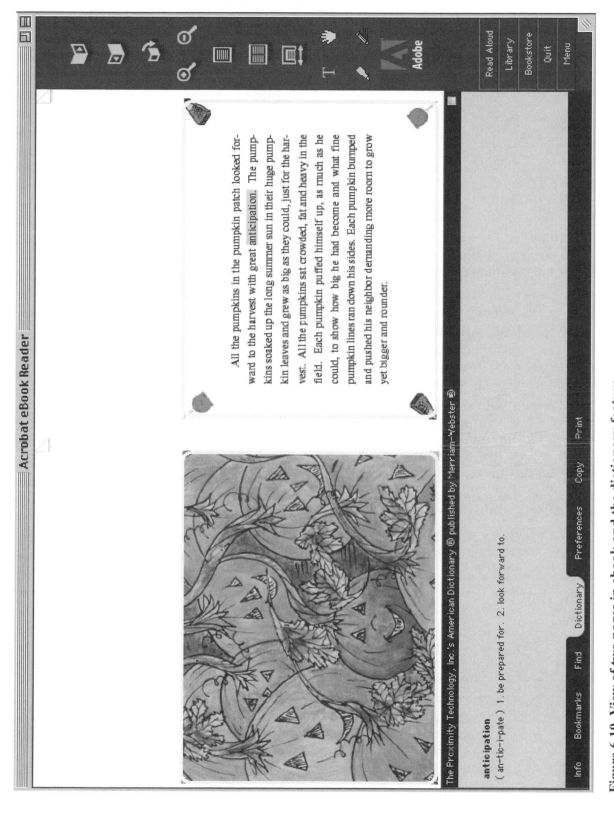

Figure 6.10 View of two pages in ebook and the dictionary feature

Author T. Cory Hansen, Illustrator Carol Foldvary-Anderson, Published by JetKor, Reno, Nevada © 2001.

ADDITIONAL RESOURCES:

Informational Web sites:

Ipicturebooks.com: **http://www.ipicturebooks.com**. This company publishes ebooks and sells them on their site. They also offer information on how to get a book published in an electronic format.

Electronic Books in Libraries: **http://www.lib.rochester.edu/main/ebooks/index.htm**. This site offers information on reading ebooks, hardware, software, and specific use as it applies to librarians.

Online Ebook Stores:

Barnes and Noble.com: **http://www.bn.com**
Amazon.com: **http://www.amazon.com**
Ebook Mall: **http://www.ebookmall.com/**. Purchase ebooks and browse through a children's section. The majority of ebooks available from this site are out-of-print books and newly published authors.
Ebook Mall Free Downloads: **http://www.ebookmall.com/free-downloads.htm**. Download free books and samples including a sample from *The Last Little Pumpkin*.
Hardshell.com: **www.hardshell.com**

Web sites with text selections:

Electronic text center at the University of Virginia: **http://etext.lib.virginia.edu/**
Project Gutenberg: **http://www.gutenberg.net**. This Web site contains classics such as *Alice in Wonderland* and *Aesop's Fables* as well as reference books.

Software and Hardware:

Ebooks can be viewed on a desktop computer, laptop, or a variety of handheld devices. Note that ebooks are published in a variety of formats. The ebook that you choose to download will specify which software it is compatible with. Here are two of the more popular software choices for reading ebook files.

- *Microsoft Reader* for Windows®: **http://www.microsoft.com/reader/info.asp**. Works on PCs and Windows® Pocket PC handhelds.

- *Adobe® Acrobat® eBook Reader*™ for Windows or Macintosh OS: **http://www.adobe.com**

Here are a couple of software choices for reading PDF, HTML, and simple text files.

- *Acrobat® Reader* for Windows or Mac OS: **http://www.adobe.com**. Reads basic PDF files.

- *Microsoft Word* for Mac® or PC, *Notepad,* or *Simpletext.* Will read Word or text files and offers a familiar reading environment.

Browsers:

These will read Web pages. User can download HTML files and read them offline.

No special ebook readers or devices required. You can use HTML ebooks with an Internet browser. They are printable and simple to navigate.

Netscape Communicator for PC or Mac®

Microsoft® Internet Explorer for PC or Mac®

Using an Ebook as an Ejournal

Almond, David. *Skellig.* New York: Delacorte Press, 1999.

OVERVIEW:

Turn an ebook into an electronic journal by teaching students how to record their responses to literature in the margins using the Annotation tool. Ebook readers like *Acrobat eBook Reader* and *Microsoft Reader* also allow the reader to bookmark pages and highlight text in different colors. In this activity, you demonstrate how to read and use an ebook on the computer and also demonstrate the features of annotation, bookmarking, and highlighting. Following the demonstration, students are given the chance to practice their new skills.

GRADE LEVEL:

3–5

MATERIALS:

Adobe eBook Reader or other Ebook Reader Software installed on your computer

Downloaded Story from Online Bookstore or from any free Web site

Overhead Projection Device

PROCEDURE:

1. Download an ebook that your students will be reading.

2. Using an overhead projection device, open the ebook program and show your students the basics of opening a book, turning pages, and accessing the menu and other tools.

   Read a chapter aloud with your students demonstrating the features of annotating, bookmarking, and highlighting. You may also want to demonstrate the features of Dictionary and Find. Discuss why you might use these specific features.

   Annotation: Annotation allows you to make notes in the margins or embedded in the text. As you are reading, thoughts may pop into your mind about a character or event, a question may arise, or you might make a personal connection to something in the book.

Highlighting: Highlighting can be useful if you are studying an informational book and you want to remember a fact or idea. Later, you can return to the ebook to find the highlighted sections.

Bookmarking: Bookmarks are similar to the paper bookmarks we use to mark where we left off or to mark an important part of a book. With *Adobe ebook Reader,* the book remembers where you stopped reading, but if there is more than one student reading the ebook, bookmarks can keep track of different people's places where they left off.

Dictionary: Most ebook readers include a dictionary where the reader can do an instant lookup of a word. Instead of interrupting your reading by getting out of your seat and finding a dictionary, get the definition quickly and move on to reading again.

Find: The Find feature allows you to search for the same word or phrase anywhere in the story. Find references to a specific character or topic of interest.

3. If this is a class read-aloud or a book that all students will be reading and you have only one computer, assign chapters to students so they can practice these specific skills. When their assigned chapter is completed, they can use the computer to read and practice the skills. If you want students to practice the skills immediately, let each student try the first chapter and when they are done, have them delete their notes and highlights for the next person. They can also mark their notes with their name and leave them within the chapter for the next student to read. If you happen to have a computer lab, students can read the book on individual computers. When placing an electronic book on multiple computers, check into copyright and pricing or find a Web site with free downloadable books and allow students to make their own selections.

In the following example, you will see a page of an ebook with notes that were made with the Annotation tool (see Figure 6.11). The student had a question about a reference to "Dr. Death" as the student was reading and the student answered the question later in the book. The student was able to go back to the question and add any new discovery to the note. The student also used the highlighting tool to highlight the passage where the question was first prompted.

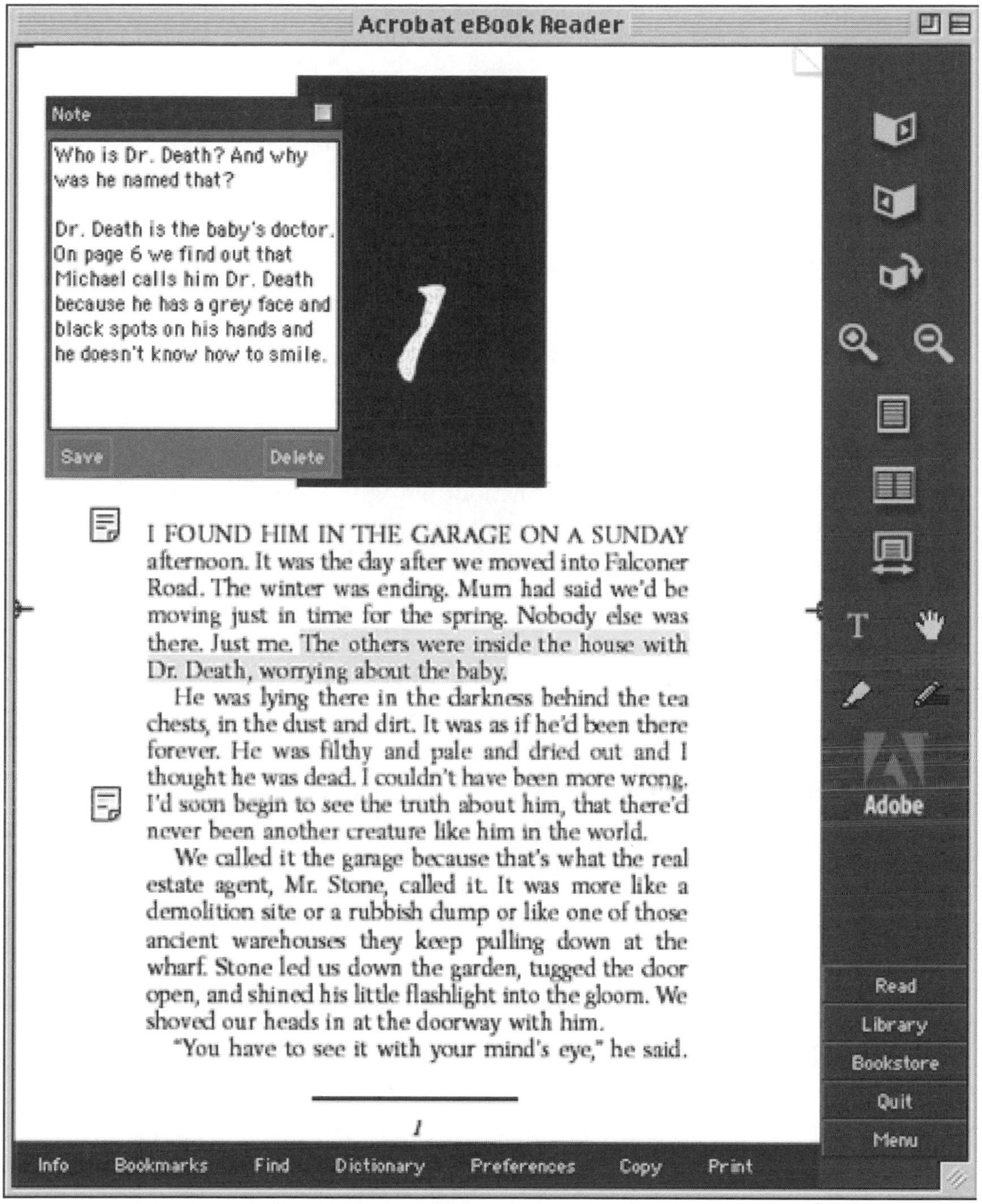

Figure 6.11 Page 1 from the ebook *Skellig* with annotation in the top left-hand corner

From SKELLIG by David Almond, copyright © 1998 by David Almond. Used by permission of Random House Children's Books, a division of Random House, Inc.

EXTENSIONS AND ADAPTATIONS:

- Create a worksheet of questions for students to complete using a variety of tools in the ebook reader. Here are some sample questions from *Skellig:*

Bookmark the page where Michael introduces Mina to Skellig.

Find any references to "27 and 53." How many times does this phrase appear? What is "27 and 53?"

Find the definitions of the following words from chapters 1–3 and write them in your own words. Demolition, mortar, and shuffled.

Who is your favorite character? Why? Answer the question using an annotation next to the paragraph where we first meet the character.

- Give exposure to ebooks by dividing your class into literature groups or book clubs at different times throughout the year and assign one of the groups an ebook selection. Allow the group to visit an online bookstore and search for their selection.

- Print out a page or chapter of the book for students to make notes on or copy and paste several sections of the book into a word processor to print. Use the excerpts for discussion and practice with comprehension skills. (Be aware that some ebooks prohibit the user from printing and copying text.)

- Leave annotations on the pages that contain questions for students to answer either in the ebook or in their reading journal.

- Discuss with your students the experience of reading an ebook. Is it easier to read a story on the computer screen or a story in a book? Which do you prefer and why?

- Using the Zoom In feature, make the text larger for students with special needs.

- Have students simply enjoy and read an ebook as they would with any book in your classroom or library.

- Place an ebook on a handheld computer and allow students to sign it out like a library book.

- Center a book discussion around an ebook. Display the ebook on an overhead projection device as students talk, and when a student refers to a particular section or page, turn to it on the computer. Have students take turns taking notes of the conversation using the Annotation tool. (Not all ebook page numbers match to the actual page numbers in the paper editions. If the page numbers do not match, use the Find feature to search for a phrase that occurs on the given page.)

ADDITIONAL RESOURCES:

See previous activity.

Using Audio Books on the Classroom Computer

Brown, Marc. *Arthur's Mystery Envelope.* New York: Little, Brown and Company, 1998.

As well as many others!!!

OVERVIEW:

The tape recorder has been the standard tool for creating a listening station. Now, though, audio files can be located on audio CDs or found just a click away on the Internet to create a computer listening station.

GRADE LEVEL:

K–5

MATERIALS:

Software to read audio files (MP3 files) (See Additional Resources.)

Audio file downloaded from Internet or audio file from audio book on CD

Book so students can read along (Optional)

Headphones for computer (Optional)

PROCEDURE:

1. Use one of the Web sites in the Additional Resources section and download an audio book file. You can also retrieve files from most audio books on CD. Be sure that you have the necessary software installed on your computer to allow you to listen to the file.

2. Create a listening station for your students by opening the necessary software and then opening the audio file. Place the book at the computer station so students can read along.

3. Instruct students on how to play the different chapters, to pause, and stop the audio file.

4. Allow students to take turns at the listening station if it is a shorter book. If it is a longer chapter book you may want to allow different groups to use the station at different times throughout the year.

EXTENSIONS AND ADAPTATIONS:

- Instead of reading along with the book as the audio file is played, have students open a painting program and draw a picture to illustrate what is going on in the book. (Other programs can be opened while an audio file is playing in the background.)

- For older students, have them open a word processing file and record their thoughts, questions, and connections as they listen to the book.

- Have students act out a chapter or section of the book as they play the audio file to the class.

- Have students create their own audio file to accompany a story they have written. Other students in the class or younger classes could then listen and read along with the published story. To do this, you will need to download the necessary software for students to create and save MP3 files.

ADDITIONAL RESOURCES:

Web Sites:

Blackstone Audiobooks.com: **http://www.blackstoneaudio.com/**. Purchase children's titles in MP3 format, regular CD format, or MP3-CD format.

Audio Books for Free.com: **http://www.audiobooksforfree.com**. This site offers a children's section of free downloadable MP3 files.

Random House Inc. Listening Library: **http://www.randomhouse.com/audio**

Harper Collins Publishers: **http://www.harperaudio.com**

Audio Books on Compact Disc, Inc.: **http://www.abcdinc.com/**. This site offers a great selection of children's literature on CDs.

AudioFile® Magazine: **http://www.audiofilemagazine.com/**. Includes children and adult reviews of audio books. The magazine is available online or a subscription can be purchased in paper format.

Mary Cavanaugh's Childrenstory.com: **http://www.childrenstory.com/**. Using the program *Real Audio,* storytellers read aloud fairy tales. Students can follow along with the words or just listen. There are also nursery rhymes, interactive stories, and holiday stories.

Software for Listening to MP3 Files:

There are several free software packages that will play MP3 and other audio file formats on your computer. The following two titles come prepackaged on Macintosh or Windows systems.

iTunes™: **http://www.apple.com/itunes**. *iTunes* gives a sampler of a few audio books. If you have an older Macintosh computer, it may have a CD player installed to play both music and audio books.

Windows® Media Player: **http://www.microsoft.com/windows/windowsmedia/download/default.asp**. This software works on both Macintosh and Windows systems. It can be downloaded at http://www.microsoft.com.

CHAPTER 7

Comprehension Strategies

Readers use a variety of strategies to decode, comprehend, and bring deeper meaning to the text they read. The more traditional method of teachers asking specific questions with one answer is no longer the only approach. This technique seems only to prove that the student has read the book, rather than focusing on how the student derived meaning from the text. Teaching students to comprehend text should begin with teacher modeling of specific strategies to assist students in independently making meaning from the text they read. Following teacher modeling, students can try using the strategies on their own. Usually, students are asked to respond in some way, whether orally, in writing, or through some artistic means.

Sticky notes are one of the essential tools used when teaching students to record their thinking from the text. They supply a way to quickly code the text without having to stop reading for too long. You will notice that some activities in this chapter involve students marking the text with their sticky notes as described and then moving to the computer to further organize their thoughts in an easy-to-read format.

This chapter is based on the comprehension strategies set forth in *Strategies that Work: Teaching Comprehension to Enhance Understanding* by Stephanie Harvey and Anne Goudvis and many other related books that discuss teaching with comprehension strategies. The activities in this chapter cover the strategies of connecting, questioning, visualizing, inferring, finding important ideas, and synthesizing. The activities can be used to introduce the strategy or to build on previous lessons.

Connecting with the Text

McLerran, Alice. *Roxaboxen*. Illustrated by Barbara Cooney. New York: Viking Penguin, 1991.

OVERVIEW:

When students can make personal connections to the books they read, they associate new meanings with the words, and the text becomes easier to read. In this activity, *Inspiration* is used to create graphic representations of the personal connections students have made to the text.

GRADE LEVEL:

3–5

MATERIALS:

Inspiration Software

Sticky Notes

Overhead Projection Device

PROCEDURE:

1. In *Inspiration*, create a template like the example provided (see Figure 7.1).

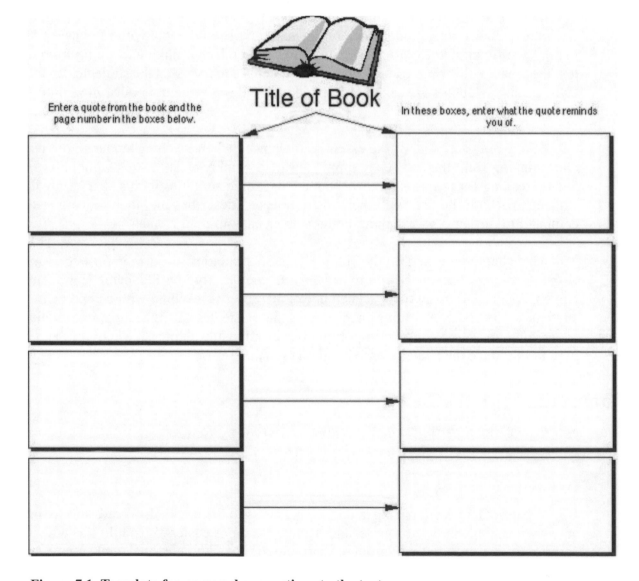

Figure 7.1 Template for personal connections to the text

This diagram was created using Inspiration® by Inspiration Software®, Inc.

2. Choose a book to read aloud that has personal connections for you.

3. As you are reading, draw attention to moments in the book that you connect to and record them using sticky notes attached to the pages. For more information on this technique, see the books in the Additional Resources section. After you finish the story, demonstrate how to input the information collected on sticky notes into the template (see Figure 7.2).

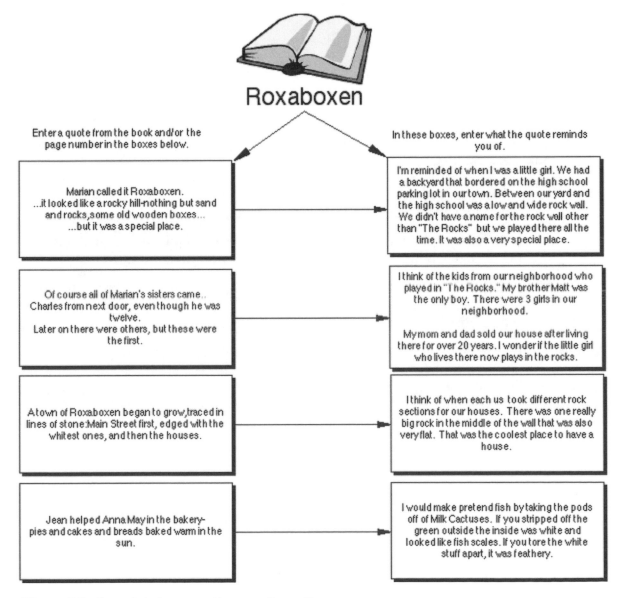

Figure 7.2 Completed personal connections diagram

This diagram was created using Inspiration® by Inspiration Software®, Inc.

4. Have students select a book with personal connections to read by themselves. As they read, have them record the personal connections they make with sticky notes.

5. After reading, have students enter the information from their sticky notes into the diagram on the computer.

6. Have students share their diagrams with a classmate or use the diagrams in reading conferences.

EXTENSIONS AND ADAPTATIONS:

- Give students sentence starters such as:

    I think of ...

    I wonder if ...

    I'm reminded of when ...

    Once I ...

Place these sentence starters in a text box within the *Inspiration* diagram so they are visible while students work.

- Print, copy, and distribute the diagram to students so they can use it for note taking as they read their book.

- If you do not have an overhead projection device connected to the computer, print the diagram and copy onto a transparency for demonstration.

- Personal connections to books help students generate wonderful writing ideas. Have students place the finished printed diagram in their writing folders for a future story.

- Create diagrams for other specific strategies such as connecting text to text, or text to world (see Figure 7.3). For more information on teaching with these strategies, see the Additional Resources section. One diagram can also be used for recording all the connections to self, text, and world.

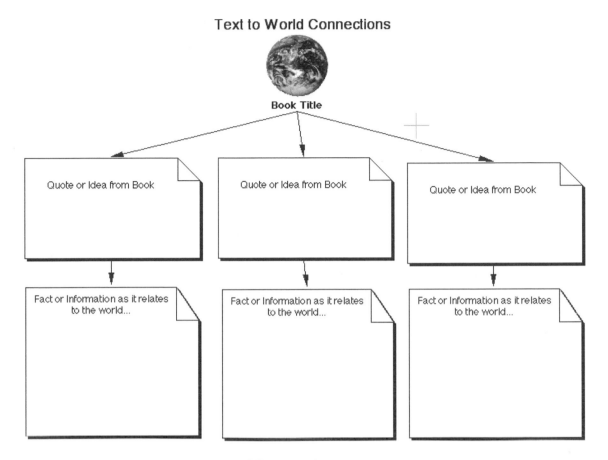

Figure 7.3 Template for text-to-world connections

This diagram was created using Inspiration® by Inspiration Software®, Inc.

ADDITIONAL RESOURCES:

Inspiration Walk-through in Appendix A

Books for making connections:

Gantos, Jack. *Joey Pigza Swallowed the Key.* New York: Farrar, Straus and Giroux, 1998.

The main character in this book has attention deficit disorder. Most children can relate to the problems he is facing and his family situation, either in their life or the life of a classmate.

Steig, William. *Amos and Boris.* New York: Farrar, Straus and Giroux, 1971.

This is a tale of friendship between a whale and a mouse.

Waber, Bernard. *Ira Sleeps Over.* Boston: Houghton Mifflin, 1972.

Students can relate to Ira's concerns when he spends his first night away from home.

Thick and Thin Questions

Bunting, Eve. *Fly Away Home.* Illustrated by Ronald Himler. New York: Clarion, 1991.

OVERVIEW:

Good readers have questions as they read. Some can be answered within the text whereas others go unanswered. This activity deals with these two kinds of questions. Using *Inspiration,* students will differentiate between the thick versus the thin questions and search for answers. In the book *Fly Away Home,* the author deals with the subject of the homeless and spurs children to ask questions.

GRADE LEVEL:

3–5

MATERIALS:

Inspiration Software

Sticky Notes or Chart Paper

Overhead Projection Device

PROCEDURE:

1. Create a template in *Inspiration* that resembles the one shown in Figure 7.4. For thick questions (global questions that evoke discussion and multiple answers), create square size shapes. For thin questions (ones that can be answered within the text or with prior knowledge), create thin long shapes. These shapes will be where the questions can later be recorded. Add thick or thin shapes attached to the questions for the answers.

   (You could also record the student's questions without a template and later change the shapes of the question and answer ideas to thick or thin shapes.)

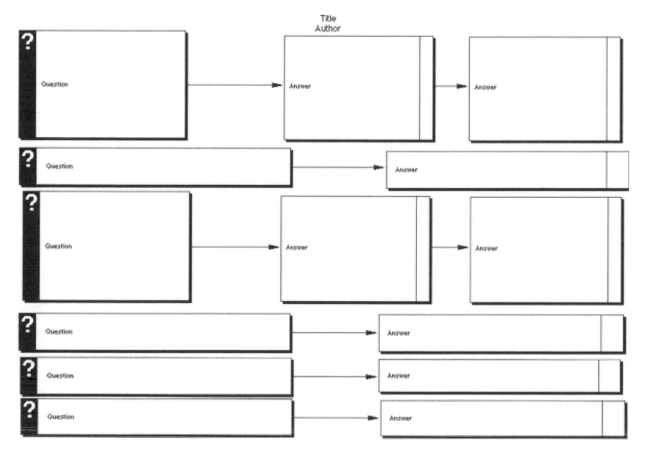

Figure 7.4 Template for thick and thin questions and answers

This diagram was created using Inspiration® by Inspiration Software®, Inc.

2. Read aloud *Fly Away Home* by Eve Bunting and ask students to raise their hands when they have a question about or related to the story. Record the questions using sticky notes in the book or on chart paper.

3. Explain to students the difference between thick and thin questions and show them the *Inspiration* diagram.

4. Record the questions in the thick or thin ideas depending on the question. Have students explain why they think the question is thick or thin.

5. On the right-hand side, record the answer(s). For thick questions, there may be several answers linked to the question. There should only be one answer for thin questions. If applicable, include the page number and quote where the answer was found. If the answer was derived from a different source describe the source (see Figure 7.5).

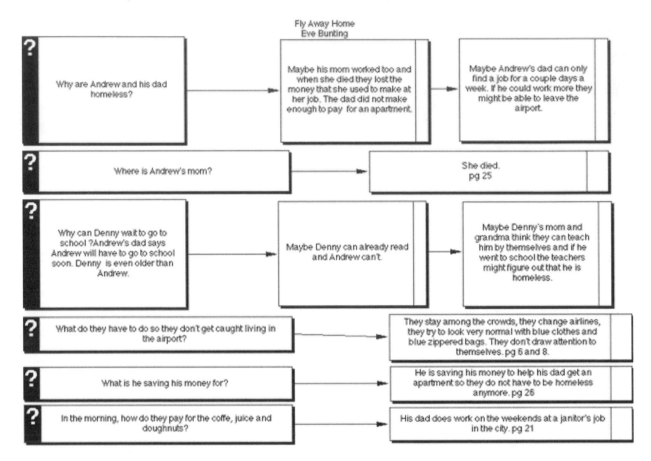

Figure 7.5 Completed thick and thin questions diagram

This diagram was created using Inspiration® by Inspiration Software®, Inc.

EXTENSIONS AND ADAPTATIONS:

- As students read, have them record questions that arise from the text in either a reading journal or on sticky notes within the book. Then have students create their own diagrams for their thick and thin questions. You can also have a book group create a thick and thin diagram.

- If available, give students two kinds of sticky notes to mark thick versus thin questions. Regular square notes can be used for thick questions and longer thin ones for the thin questions. Rather than differentiating between the questions during the discussion, students can make a distinction between the questions as they read.

- Print out an empty template for students to fill in as they read.

- To simplify the activity, have students diagram all their questions and answers in a two-column format without differentiating between thick and thin questions.

- Instead of diagramming thick and thin questions, create a question web that centers around one question. Place one global or thick question in the main idea and record all the possibilities in ideas that link to the main idea (see Figure

7.6). Have students work on this individually or record the answers during a class discussion. Take this one step further by having students answer global questions in a round-robin format using *Inspiration*. See "Synthesizing through a Round Robin Journal" for more information on how to conduct a round robin with technology.

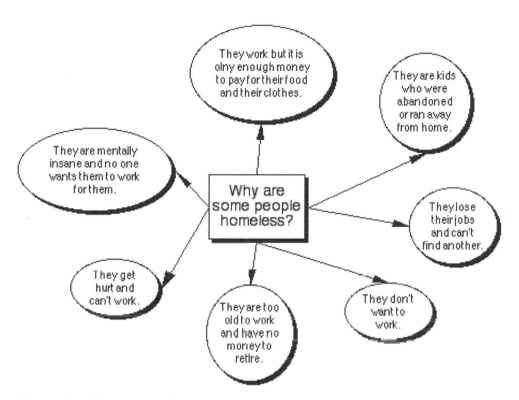

Figure 7.6 Global question web
This diagram was created using Inspiration® by Inspiration Software®, Inc.

ADDITIONAL RESOURCES:

Inspiration Walk-through in Appendix A

Books for Questioning:

Almond, David. *Skellig.* New York: Delacorte Press, 1999.

Who is Skellig? This book abounds with questions about the mysterious character.

McDonald, Megan. *The Potato Man.* New York: Orchard Books, 1991.

The children who live in the neighborhood constantly tease the potato vendor. Why are they so mean?

"Drawing" Comparisons

Baron, Kathy. *The Tree of Time.* Yosemite National Park, CA: Yosemite Association, 1994.

OVERVIEW:

When we visualize from fiction, we create the characters, settings, and specific scenes in our minds through our own background knowledge and imagination. With nonfiction, visualizing occurs when there are comparisons that deal with the measurements of time, distance, length, size, and weight. Many nonfiction books include illustrations that draw comparisons between these concepts. Technology may not be the best tool when asking students to visualize with fiction, but it can be very helpful when visualizing with nonfiction because illustrations such as graphs, charts, and timelines can be created easily with software. In this activity, students will create a scaled drawing to accompany a book about the famous Wawona sequoia tree.

GRADE LEVEL:

3–5

MATERIALS:

Drawing Software with grid *(AppleWorks Drawing* or *Microsoft Word)*

Objects of various heights for comparison

PROCEDURE:

1. Begin by reading aloud the book to your students. At the end of the book, inform students that the Wawona tree was 234 feet high when it fell. Discuss how big that is. (Throughout the book, there is a time comparison of historical events to the growth of the giant sequoia. The height comparison you will be asking students to make is not made in the book.)

2. Generate a list of five or six objects for comparison to the tree. Using the Internet or other resources, locate the heights of these objects. (You could also have students generate a list of objects they think might be bigger or smaller than the tree.)

Heights of Various Objects:

Wawona tree-234 feet

Eiffel Tower-986 feet

Our school-30 feet

Brachiosaurus-50 feet

Third-grade student-4 feet

3. Post the list of objects and their heights or photocopy the list and distribute to students.

4. Have students open a drawing program that has a grid on the screen. Explain to them that each square on the grid will be equal to 40 feet. (You may wish to change the scale based on the size of the grid you are using.) In *AppleWorks,* the grid is there by default, but in *Microsoft Word* you need to add it using the Draw tool. Search under the Help menu to locate directions for adding the grid. (If students are not familiar with scale, teach the concept before this lesson.)

5. Allow time for students to draw the objects side by side using the drawing tools (see Figure 7.7).

6. When finished, have students print their completed comparison.

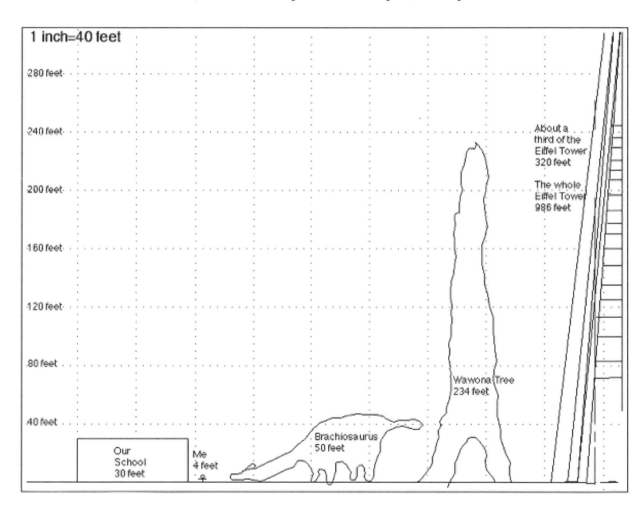

Figure 7.7 Scaled comparison drawing

EXTENSIONS AND ADAPTATIONS:

- Younger students benefit from doing a physical measurement first. Go out on the playground and have your students drag out a string to measure 234 feet so they can visualize the distance.

- Create a template for students by typing the scale (1 inch = 40 feet) on the drawing document and creating a scale going up the left-hand side for each 40 feet increment. This will make it easier for students to determine the heights of the objects on the page.

- Have students compare only two objects rather than many.

- Don't forget that spreadsheet programs are great for visualizing in nonfiction because graphs and charts can be created.

- Scaled maps are a great way to visualize the setting of a book from specific details that the author may have supplied (great for historical fiction).

- The simplest artistic response for visualization of a scene or character from fiction is drawing it on paper or on the computer.

- Instead of you doing the fact finding, older students could generate their own list of objects, and using the Internet, find out the heights of each for their size comparison. Each student's comparisons will be different and interesting to share.

- To make the assignment more difficult, have students record the width of each of the bases of the objects and make sure their drawing is to scale with both height and width.

ADDITIONAL RESOURCES:

Building Big: **http://www.buildingbig.com**. This site is based on the book, *Building Big* by David McCauley. It offers information about tunnels, bridges, and buildings including dimensions.

Zoom Dinosaurs.com: **http://www.enchantedlearning.com/subjects/dinosaurs/**

Books for Visualizing:

Day, Alexandra. *Good Dog Carl.* New York: Scholastic, 1985.

This is a wordless picture book that sparks the imagination of the reader.

Zolotow, Charlotte. *The Seashore Book.* New York: HarperCollins, 1992.

A mother describes the seashore to her little boy as he tries to imagine what it looks like.

Inferences Using *Inspiration*

Van Allsburg, Chris. *The Stranger.* Boston: Houghton Mifflin, 1986.

OVERVIEW:

Through pictures and text, readers can infer what the characters may be feeling or other important details of the story. Inferring is similar to predicting except that when you predict an outcome to a story, you can have a definitive answer to whether the prediction was true or not. With inferring, it is more like an educated guess. In this activity, you model the skill of inferring with a read-aloud and then have students practice the skill on their own. Similar to the activity in this chapter where students made personal connections, students use *Inspiration* to record the inferences they make.

GRADE LEVEL:

3–5

MATERIALS:

Inspiration Software

Collection of picture books that are good for making inferences

Sticky Notes

Overhead Projection Device

1. In *Inspiration,* create a template like the one shown in Figure 7.8. Notice the two rectangles to the right side of the diagram that say "Confirmed" and "Contradicted." These are a key for the further labeling of the inferences once they are made. The rectangles were created by locating the positive and negative signs in the Symbol Palette. See step 6 for more direction on how students can use the key.

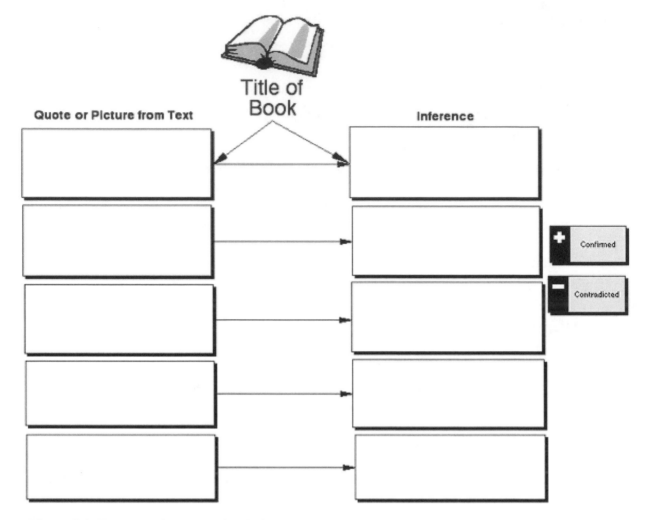

Figure 7.8 Template for recording inferences

This diagram was created using Inspiration® by Inspiration Software®, Inc.

2. Gather together a collection of books that are great for making inferences. (Chris Van Allsburg books are especially great!) From this collection, choose a book to read aloud.

3. As you are reading, draw attention to pictures or words in the book where you can infer something about the story or characters and record the inferences using sticky notes attached to the pages. For more information on this technique, see the books in the Additional Resources section. When you have finished the story, demonstrate how to input the information collected on sticky notes into the template.

4. Have students select a book to read by themselves or with partners. As they read, have them record the inferences they make with sticky notes.

5. After reading, have students enter the information from their sticky notes into the diagram on the computer. In the next example, the students drew some inferences that were probably not true because the stranger in the book was most likely Jack

Frost. Whether right or wrong, placing their thoughts into a linear diagram allows the teacher to better evaluate their thinking as they progressed through the book (see Figure 7.9).

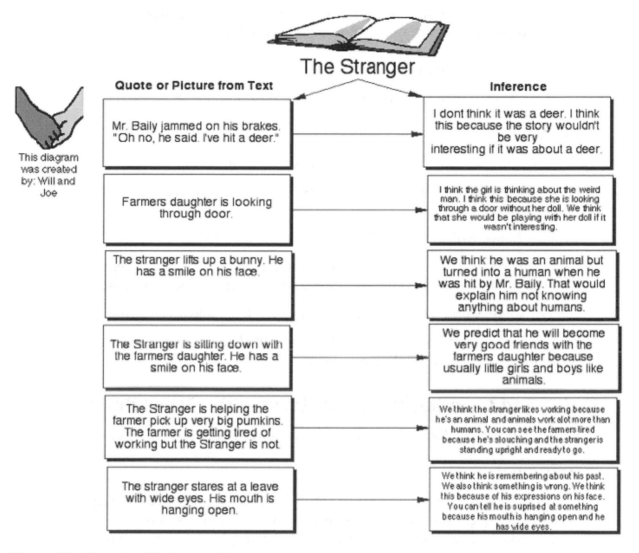

Figure 7.9 Completed inference diagram

This diagram was created using Inspiration® by Inspiration Software®, Inc.

6. (Optional) Using the key on the side of the diagram, change the inferences boxes in the second column to either a positive or negative sign to indicate whether the inference was contradicted or confirmed. Some inferences will be neither confirmed nor contradicted. The positive and negative signs can be found in the Number section of the Symbol Palette.

7. Have students share their completed diagrams with a classmate or use the diagrams in reading conferences.

EXTENSIONS AND ADAPTATIONS:

- Print, copy, and distribute the diagram to students so they can use it for note taking as they read their book.

- If you do not have an overhead projection device connected to the computer, print the diagram and copy onto a transparency.

ADDITIONAL RESOURCE:

Inspiration Walk-through in Appendix A

Books:

Hazen, Barbara Shook. *Tight Times.* New York: Viking, 1979.

The pictures and words allow readers to draw many inferences about a family facing tight times.

Sachar, Louis. *Holes.* New York: Random House, Inc., 1998.

This story builds with small clues as to the mystery of the prison camp. Readers can infer from the moment the reading begins to the final moments of the story.

Van Allsburg, Chris. *The Wreck of the Zephyr.* Boston: Houghton Mifflin, 1983.

Students can make their first inference at the beginning of the story as they wonder why the wreckage of a boat is high on a hill.

Locating and Creating Important Ideas with a Word Processor

Lineker, Gary. *The Young Soccer Player.* New York: DK Publishing, Inc., 1994.

OVERVIEW:

Determining importance in reading is central to learning from reading. Nonfiction is particularly good for teaching students how to find the essential or most important ideas in the text because it is informational to begin with. Nonfiction has a way of identifying important ideas through the styles of the text, headings and subheadings, and other cues. The students have to be able to find these cues to learn. The cues can be differing fonts, lists, bulleting, italic, bold, cue words and phrases, captions, labels, illustrations, and graphics. In this activity, students will explore the conventions of nonfiction and create their own nonfiction page about a topic of interest.

GRADE LEVEL:

2–5

MATERIALS:

Word Processing or Drawing Software *(AppleWorks* or *Microsoft Word)*

Examples of nonfiction books that demonstrate conventions of nonfiction

I Found ... Reproducible (See Figure 7.11.)

My Topic is ... Reproducible (See Figure 7.12.)

PROCEDURE:

1. Surround your students with nonfiction materials.

2. Over time, discuss and demonstrate nonfiction conventions through reading aloud different nonfiction examples. Examples of nonfiction conventions can be found on either reproducible.

3. Have students examine several books and find conventions of nonfiction. Copy and distribute the **I Found ...** reproducible for students to complete for two books.

4. Explain to students that they will each be creating a page on a particular topic. Their page needs to include at least three of the conventions that have been discussed.

5. Copy and distribute the **My Topic is ...** reproducible and have students choose a topic that they are very interested in.

6. Have students research their topic and decide what they will include on their page. Require that students include at least three of the conventions in their draft of the page. They can check these off on the **My Topic is ...** reproducible. On the back of the reproducible they should plan what the page will look like.

7. Have students use a word processing or drawing program and type in the information. They can change the fonts, sizes, and styles to highlight the headings and use any other word processing skills to show the important ideas.

8. Last, have them insert any graphics, charts, or illustrations that add to the text (see Figure 7.10).

9. Print out the completed pages and share with fellow classmates.

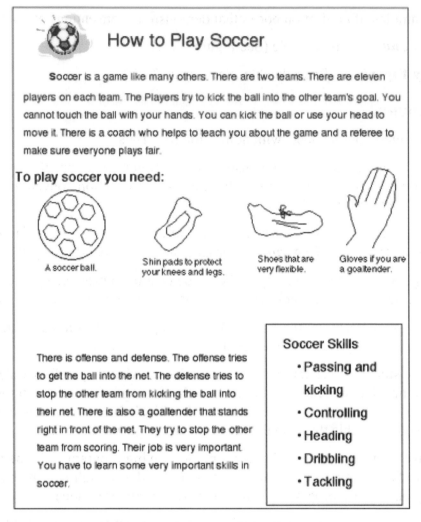

Figure 7.10 Student example of nonfiction conventions in writing

EXTENSIONS AND ADAPTATIONS:

- Have older students create more pages on the topic.

- Give students a short selection of text from a book or magazine article. Type the file in a word processing program and save as a template. Have students edit the selection by adding and changing any fonts, sizes, and styles that better identify the important ideas. Take the activity one step further by asking students to add a graphic (map, chart, graph, or labeled illustration) to accompany the selection.

- Use an ebook to demonstrate to students how to properly highlight information in nonfiction or to add notes in the margins. See Chapter 6, "Using an Ebook as an Ejournal," for more information on the capabilities of ebooks.

ADDITIONAL RESOURCE:

Saving Templates Walk-through in Appendix A

Book Title:

Author:

I found these non-fiction conventions:

☐ Bold

☐ Italics

☐ Underlining

☐ Bulleted List

☐ Larger fonts for headings

☐ Graph

☐ Illustration

☐ Labels

☐ Captions

☐ Maps

☐ Photos

Book Title:

Author:

I found these non-fiction conventions:

☐ Bold

☐ Italics

☐ Underlining

☐ Bulleted List

☐ Larger fonts for headings

☐ Graph

☐ Illustration

☐ Labels

☐ Captions

☐ Maps

☐ Photos

Figure 7.11 I Found ... Reproducible

Name:

My topic is:

Why I chose this topic:

I am going to include these non-fiction conventions:

☐ Bold   ☐ Graph

☐ Italics   ☐ Illustration

☐ Underlining   ☐ Labels

☐ Bulleted List   ☐ Captions

☐ Larger fonts for   ☐ Maps
  headings
                              ☐ Photos

Sketch the layout on the back of this page.

Figure 7.12 My Topic Is … Reproducible

Synthesizing through a Round Robin Journal

El Nabli, Dina. "Bush Proposes New Government Department." *Time for Kids.com* (June 7, 2002): **http://www.timeforkids.com/TFK/news/story**

OVERVIEW:

When students synthesize they form a new idea or new perspective. They combine the knowledge they already have with the knowledge they gain through reading. Synthesizing is the hardest of comprehension strategies to teach. The reader needs to be able to use all the previous strategies (Connecting, Questioning, Visualizing, Inferring, and Determining Important Ideas) to be able to synthesize text. Therefore, the skill of synthesizing cannot be taught until students have competency in the other strategies.

In this activity, students are asked to respond to a current events article from a popular children's magazine using the strategies they previously learned. Although the example does not take the form of a traditional book, it is literature that we should be asking students to read and respond to. In the case of this activity, the response involves a creative use of technology.

GRADE LEVEL:

3–5

MATERIALS:

Word Processing Software

4 computers

Short Text Selection

Overhead Projection Device (Optional)

PROCEDURE:

1. Prepare four or more computers with a word processing template that includes an article that students will be responding to. If the article was obtained from the Internet, it can be copied and pasted to a word processing program. If not, you will need to type it and save as a template. Create signs labeled 1, 2, 3, and 4 and post these on the top of the prepared computers stations.

2. Read the article aloud to your class on an overhead projection device if possible. You can also have students follow along on the Internet or using the templates you created.

   (In the example, the article was found at http://www.timeforkids.com and discussed the president's request to Congress for a new department to protect Americans from terrorism.)

3. Explain to students that they will be using all the strategies they learned during the year to respond to the article. What connections do they make? What questions do they have? Can they draw any inferences? What about visualizing? What were the important ideas or themes that arose from the article?

4. Next, discuss the protocol for responding and moving through the four stations in groups. Students will have 5 minutes at each station to respond to the article. When the timer sounds, remind students to finish their last thought, save, and move to the next station. When they move to the next station, they should read what the last group wrote and either respond to the comments from a previous group or add new comments that may have arisen from the ideas of others. Conversing in this way helps students to clear up misconceptions, find answers to questions, and connect their feelings with others.

5. Divide students into groups to begin the round robin response.

6. When the timer rings for the round robin to stop, have students do a final save and print the file.

Sample from Round Robin Conversation:

I saw the president speak on T.V.

The president must think that Tom Ridge is doing a good job if he wants to give him a cabinet position.

We think he thought of the warning system.

What is the warning system?

I heard about this on the news. If it helps to protect Americans then it is probably a good thing.

I wonder how Congress feels about this? What will they do?

Do you think the president knew there was a threat to the United States before September 11th?

No, if he did then he would have done more.

We think he knew something, but he gets a lot of warnings so they have to be careful which ones to listen to.

I think other people in the government had warnings but they were not passed on to their superiors.

I wonder how the other departments feel about this? Do some of them work together right now anyway?

Yes, we think that the CIA and FBI have to work together sometimes. Someone saw it in a movie.

The article does not mention the FBI and the CIA. I think these would stay the same. They would not become a part of the new department.

We think that some agencies have more power than others. Who would have the most power?

It might be equal.

7. Have a class discussion. Were there any questions that were never answered? Was there a particular idea that made people really connect? What ideas continued to arise again and again? As students discuss the experience, they are beginning to synthesize.

8. Copy the responses for each student. Give time for students to review the lists and write a summary of their final thoughts or synthesis on the selection. Students can use pencil and paper or a word processing program.

Sample of one student's final synthesis:

After reading and talking about this article, I think the Congress should pass this bill. We have to do everything we can to protect people and times are very different than they used to be. I think that Tom Ridge would gain a lot more power if he was a cabinet member and he could make more of a difference. It sounds like a very big job to head that many departments. Because the FBI and the CIA are not going to be part of this bigger department, than I think the president needs to do something about these organizations. They made some mistakes before September 11th, and the people responsible should be fired. I am scared that there might be another attack so the government needs to organize!

EXTENSIONS AND ADAPTATIONS:

- After the four rotations, have students return to their first station to further mark the responses. For connections, use **T-S**, text to self, **T-T**, text to text, and **T-W**, text to world. Place a **Q** next to questions, an **I** next to inferences, a **V** for visualizing, and an **IMP** for important ideas.

- If the article is online, have students move back and forth between their Internet browser and the word processing program when they need to read or respond in writing.

- Guide students with more specific prompts at each computer station. For example, "What questions would you have for the president of the United States?" or "How would you better protect Americans from the threat of terrorism?"

- For visualizing, open a drawing program on one of the stations and allow students to create an illustration.

- For younger students this kind of activity might be more appropriate with a topic that you are about to introduce. Try a KWL (What I **Know,** What I **Want** to Know, What I **Learned**) with this round robin technique. Start with four questions that prompt students to tell what they know about various aspects of a topic. For emergent or nonreaders, use *Kid Pix* or another painting program so students can respond with words, stamps, or their own drawings.

- Use *Inspiration* to conduct a round robin brainstorm. Place a topic, question, or prompt in the main idea on four computer stations. Have students rotate through the stations adding new ideas to the web.

- Have groups select a font or color that identifies their group as they respond. At the next station, they will need to remember the font they used to remain consistent.

- Encourage students to copy and paste phrases from the text selection to accompany their comments.

- Use an excerpt from fiction or a poem instead of a current events article.

- When students are comfortable with the round robin on computers, they may be ready to have a similar dialogue online. See Chapter 5, "Book Chats," for more information on online dialogues.

ADDITIONAL RESOURCES:

Copy, Paste, and Online Clip-art Walk-through in Appendix

Short Text Selections or Magazines:

Time for Kids:

Time Inc., Time-Life Building, 1271 Avenue of the Americas, New York, NY 10020–1393

Cricket:

The Cricket Magazine Group, P.O. Box 7434, Red Oak, IA 51591–0434

CHAPTER 8

Technology Across the Curriculum

The picture book is the perfect medium to introduce students to a topic for the first time in a very visual way. This chapter takes a theme or unit and develops technology-related activities to demonstrate how literature and technology can be a vehicle for learning about virtually any topic of interest. Three books were chosen to illustrate technology activities in the curricular areas of math, science, and social studies. For each book, there are two activities. Following the activities are lists of additional ideas to further use technology across the curriculum.

Math—*The Greedy Triangle*

Burns, Marilyn. *The Greedy Triangle.* Illustrated by Gordon Silveria. New York: Scholastic Inc., 1994.

The triangle loves hanging out on rooftops or in the small space that is created when people put their hands on their hips. He gets bored, though, and changes into a square. He discovers new places to go with his new shape but loses interest again. He continues to change until he has so many sides he doesn't know what to do. He finally decides that being a triangle was very good and returns to his original shape. This book deals with shapes in a creative way as well as teaching a lesson about being happy with who you are.

Finding Shapes in the Real World

OVERVIEW:

The greedy triangle could become part of a sailboat, a half sandwich, or the roof on a house. Using the technology of photography with a drawing program, students will create pictures that combine real-life examples of shapes with a bit of creativity.

GRADE LEVEL:

K–5

MATERIALS:

Painting or Drawing Software *(Kid Pix Studio Deluxe)*

Digital Camera or Scanner

PROCEDURE:

1. Read aloud *The Greedy Triangle* or another book about shapes.

2. Assign different shapes to individual students or allow students to choose the shape they think is the most fun to be.

3. Have students think of places where their shape occurs in the real world.

4. Have students bring in pictures of real-world examples of shapes or go on a field trip to take digital pictures of shapes in the real world. If the pictures are not in a digital format, scan the pictures.

5. Once in digital format, have students individually import their picture into a drawing program (see Figure 8.1). The "Import" or "Insert" command can usually be found within the File menu.

Figure 8.1 Digital picture of dumbbell imported into *Kid Pix*

6. With the painting or drawing tools, have students illustrate their "living" shape over the spot where it occurs in the picture. Refer to *The Greedy Triangle* and the illustrations in the book for students to get an idea of the final product.

7. Below the picture, have students type a sentence explaining what it is like to be the shape when it is part of the real-world object. For example, in the book the triangle liked hanging out in the small triangle that forms when people put their hands on their hips because he could listen to their conversation (see Figure 8.2).

8. Have students print out their pictures and display them on a classroom bulletin board.

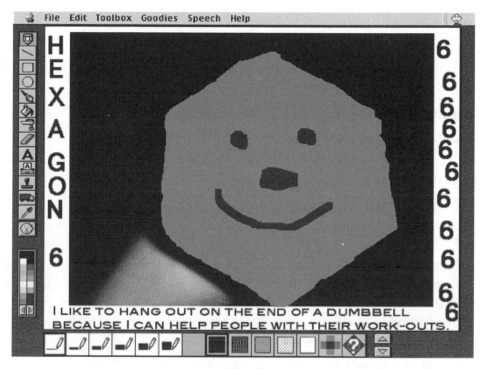

Figure 8.2 Digital picture with incorporated illustration and sentence
Taken from Kid Pix® Studio. ©Broderbund Properties LLC. Used with permission.

EXTENSIONS AND ADAPTATIONS:

- Combine each student's drawing into a class slideshow.

- Create a file with a picture that has many shapes within it. Have students use the drawing tools to outline where they find the different shapes.

ADDITIONAL RESOURCES:

Kid Pix Walk-through in Appendix A

Kid Pix Planning Sheet in Appendix B

Shapes Presentation

OVERVIEW:

In this activity, students will create a multimedia presentation that teaches other classmates about the different shapes.

GRADE LEVEL:

K–5

MATERIALS:

Multimedia or Slideshow Software *(Hyperstudio, Kid Pix Slideshow, AppleWorks* or *Microsoft Powerpoint)*

Multimedia Planning Sheet Reproducible in Appendix B

Overhead Projection Device

PROCEDURE:

1. Read aloud *The Greedy Triangle* or another book about shapes.

2. Assign the shapes in *The Greedy Triangle* to pairs of students.

3. Using planning sheets, have each pair of students create two cards for their presentation. The first card should have a picture of the single shape with its name and a definition. The second card should have an example of where the shape can be found in real life. If you wish, use the example to show students what a completed *Hyperstudio* stack would look like (see Figures 8.3 and 8.4).

4. Give students enough time to complete their work on the computer.

5. Allow students time to share their completed stacks with the rest of the class.

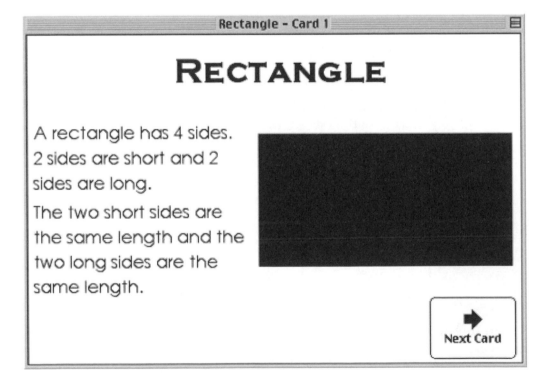

Figure 8.3 Card 1 in shapes presentation
Hyperstudio® and all of its screen images are a registered trademark of Knowledge Adventure, Inc. and are used under license.

Figure 8.4 Card 2 in shapes presentation

Hyperstudio® and all of its screen images are a registered trademark of Knowledge Adventure, Inc. and are used under license.

EXTENSIONS AND ADAPTATIONS:

- Take each group's shape presentation and combine them into one large shape presentation for other classes to use as a learning tool.

- Have students record themselves reading aloud the definitions.

- Keep younger student presentations to one card and lengthen older students' presentations to more than two by having them find several instances where the shape occurs in real life.

ADDITIONAL RESOURCE:

Hyperstudio Walk-through in Appendix A

Other Ideas:

- Have students create a spreadsheet to organize information about the different shapes. In the first column, type "Name of Shape." In the second column, type "Number of Sides." In the third column, type "Number of Angles," and in the fourth column, type "Example in Real Life." Change the categories according to the grade level and your objectives.

- Place the same information in the just mentioned spreadsheet idea into a database. Create fields according to the example and include a field for a picture of the shape.

- Create manipulatives using the computer. Draw various shapes and have students arrange them to form a picture.

Social Studies—*So You Want to Be President*

St. George, Judith. *So You Want to Be President.* Illustrated by David Small. New York: Penguin Putnam Books, 2000.

This book teaches presidential facts in a humorous way. It discusses the good and the not-so-good things about being a president of the United States. It also gives specific and little known facts about the previous presidents. For example, did you know that eight presidents grew up in log cabins?

The Good and the Bad

OVERVIEW:

As the book describes, there are good and bad things about being the president of the United States. Begin a discussion on this topic and then have students create their own diagrams illustrating what they believe is the good and the bad.

GRADE LEVEL:

3–5

MATERIALS:

Inspiration Software

Overhead Projection Device

PROCEDURE:

1. Read aloud *So You Want to Be President* by Judith St. George.

2. Discuss with students the good and bad things about being the president.

3. Have students open *Inspiration* and create a diagram that illustrates the good versus the bad things about being the president. At the top of the page, have them use the main idea bubble to type a title as in the example. Connected to the title, have them create two ideas that say "The Good" and "The Bad." Students should record their ideas and connect them to either "The Good" or "The Bad" ideas (see Figure 8.5).

4. Have students print out their finished diagrams.

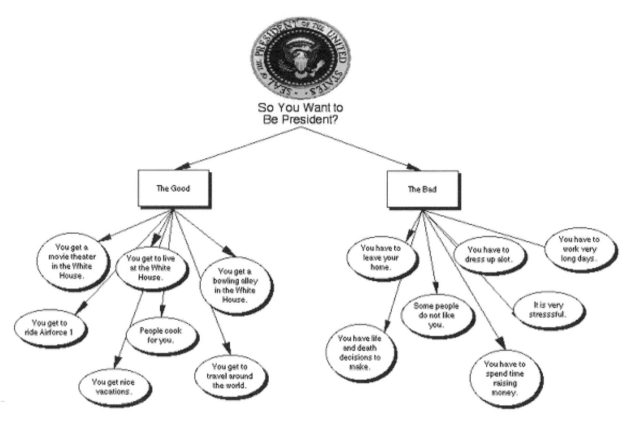

Figure 8.5 Completed student diagram

This diagram was created using Inspiration® by Inspiration Software®, Inc.

5. Share the student diagrams as a class or with partners to see the differences and new ideas that students generated.

EXTENSIONS AND ADAPTATIONS:

*   Create a template ahead of time and ask students to fill in the bubbles with their ideas.

*   Have students convert the diagram to an outline format by clicking on the "Outline" button in the upper left-hand corner of the screen. Have them print the outline to use as a guide for writing an essay on the good and bad of being a president.

*   Have students think about other members of the presidential family such as the spouse or children. What would be the good and bad things about their roles?

ADDITIONAL RESOURCE:

Inspiration Walk-through in Appendix A

A Day in the Life of the President

OVERVIEW:

What would it be like to be president for a day? What does the president's daily schedule look like? Use the Internet and other resources for the students to conduct research on the president and his daily or weekly schedules. Using the information they find, have them create an imaginary day in the life timeline using the program *TimeLiner*.

GRADE LEVEL:

4–5

MATERIALS:

TimeLiner Software

PROCEDURE:

1. Read aloud *So You Want to Be President* by Judith St. George.

2. Have students research online and in books what the president's daily or weekly schedule typically looks like. Refer to the Web sites in the Additional Resources section.

3. To begin a timeline, have your students open the program *TimeLiner* and choose **Floating Timeline.** A floating timeline allows the student to type in times of day rather than individual dates.

4. In the "When" column have students type the times of day. In the "What" column have students type what the president is doing. "What" the President is doing can be based on a real day's events or can be based on an imaginary day (see Figure 8.6).

	When	What
	7 AM	President wakes up and has breakfast.
	8 AM	President meets with his cabinet.
	10 AM	President meets with some Senators about a new law.
	11:30 AM	President has a quick lunch.
	12 PM	President flies to New York City to go to a cermemony at Ground Zero.
	3 PM	President makes a speech to workers at Ground Zero.
	4 PM	President meets with the MAyor of New York City.
	5 PM	President has his supper on Air Force One.
	6 PM	President flies to Crawford, Texas to visit his ranch with his wife.
	7 PM	President hangs out with his wife and animals and relaxes before his next busy day.
	9 PM	President goes to bed

Figure 8.6 View of data format

5. When students have entered all the daily events into the program, they can convert the data into small banner format by clicking on the third button in the top row of small buttons (see Figure 8.7).

Figure 8.7 Buttons to choose various formats in *Timeliner*

6. Have students format their small banner by changing the fonts and adding a title. To add a title, locate the command "New title ..." under the Edit menu. Encourage students to add graphics to their timelines (see Figure 8.8).

A Day in the President's Life

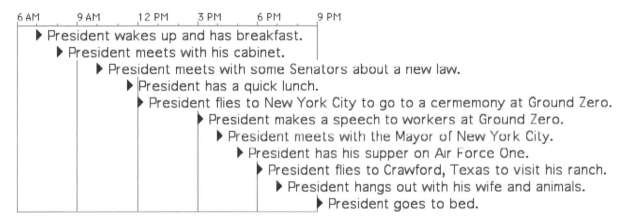

Figure 8.8 Completed timeline of a day in the life of a president

These timelines were created using TimeLiner ™ 5.0 by Tom Snyder Productions.

EXTENSIONS AND ADAPTATIONS:

• Instead of a day in the life, have students create a timeline showing a weekly schedule of the president. Have students base the schedule from a real week in the president's life, or they can create events based on their research.

• If you do not have access to the program *TimeLiner,* use a drawing or painting program to create a finished timeline.

ADDITIONAL RESOURCES:

The White House: **http://www.whitehouse.gov**. Find press secretary briefings that detail some of the president's schedule.

The White House Historical Association: **http://www.whitehousehistory.org/**. This site has a learning center with activities and lesson plans for students and teachers.

Mr. President: Profiles of our Nation's Leaders: **http://educate.si.edu/president/**

Other Ideas:

- Create a class database to organize presidential information. Include fields like President name, Rank, Term, Political Party, Spouse, Birth Date, Death Date, and so on.

- After students have researched a specific president, have them create a multimedia presentation on interesting facts about his life and presidency.

- Create a character diagram in *Inspiration* on the inner and outer characteristics of one president. (This is similar to the activity in Chapter 1, "Inner Versus Outer Characteristics.")

- Using *Inspiration,* compare and contrast two different presidencies.

- There are presidential caricatures throughout the book. Talk about what a caricature is and have students try their hand at creating their own caricatures of famous people, presidents, or even classmates. Use the Internet to do research on the history of political caricatures or try the Caricature Zone Web site. The site has a section where you can create a caricature by selecting various attributes of the face, ears, and hair. Caricature Zone: **http://www.magixl.com/heads/index.html**

- Have students do research on one president and create a timeline of the important events in his life using *TimeLiner* by Tom Snyder Productions.

- Have students pretend they are president. What types of laws would they pass or what kinds of decisions would they make. What are their presidential policies regarding education, welfare, and so forth. Have students put their ideas into a multimedia slideshow format.

Science—*Snowflake Bentley*

Martin, Jacqueline Briggs. *Snowflake Bentley.* Illustrated by Mary Azarian. Boston: Houghton Mifflin Company, 1998.

This is a beautiful biography about a man nicknamed Snowflake Bentley who loved nature and the mystery of snowflakes. He grew up on a farm in Vermont and through his explorations learned how to photograph a single snowflake.

How a Snowflake Is Formed

OVERVIEW:

Inspiration is great for diagramming scientific processes. It allows students to have a better visual understanding and requires them to break down a concept into smaller parts.

GRADE LEVEL:

2–5

MATERIALS:

Inspiration Software

Overhead Projection Device

PROCEDURE:

1. Read aloud *Snowflake Bentley* by Jacqueline Briggs Martin.

2. Have students conduct research on how a snowflake is formed using the Internet or books including *Snowflake Bentley.* It may be helpful to have students conduct their research in small groups rather than individually. Have students take notes on the different steps.

3. Using an overhead projection device, open the program *Inspiration* and as a class have students contribute their findings to a diagram on the formation of a snowflake. As students contribute the various steps, create new ideas on the screen. Some flexibility will be necessary as some information may need to be combined into one step while other information may need to be inserted as different groups contribute.

4. Connect the ideas to each other in the order they occur.

5. Format the diagram by adding a title. You can also use different weather graphics in the Symbol Palette to change the shape of the ideas (see Figure 8.9).

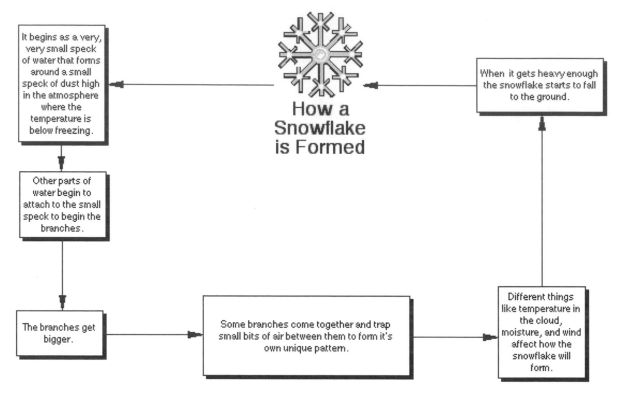

Figure 8.9 Completed diagram of how a snowflake is formed

This diagram was created using Inspiration® by Inspiration Software®, Inc.

6. Have students use the diagram to write a fictional story from the perspective of a snowflake forming and falling to the earth. Have them use a word processing program to publish their final draft. The story should include information like how does it feel to be a snowflake as it forms, what their final shape is, and what they end up being used for.

EXTENSIONS AND ADAPTATIONS:

- In this activity, one group discovered that different conditions led to different shapes and wanted to describe the formations of the different classifications of snowflakes. They were encouraged to create an additional *Inspiration* diagram that showed the different paths the snowflakes could take to form each type of snowflake.

ADDITIONAL RESOURCES:

Inspiration Walk-through in Appendix A

Bentley, W. A., and W. J. Humphreys. *Snow Crystals*. New York: Dover Publications, Inc., 1962.

Virtual Tour of the Snowflake Bentley Museum

OVERVIEW:

Although it might be difficult for some classes to take a bus to Vermont and visit the Snowflake Bentley Museum, any class with Internet access can take a virtual field trip by logging onto the Web site.

GRADE LEVEL:

K–5

MATERIALS:

Snowflake Bentley Museum: **http://snowflakebentley.com/museum.htm**

Overhead Projection Device

Virtual Field Trip Log Reproducible (See Figure 8.10.)

PROCEDURE:

1. Read aloud *Snowflake Bentley* by Jacqueline Briggs Martin.

2. Use an overhead projection device to demonstrate how to logon to the Snowflake Bentley Museum Web site. Demonstrate for students how to access the different information available on the Web site. (This Web site has a photograph of the inside of the museum where you can click on an object or photograph and get a closer look.)

3. Give students a chance to visit the museum individually or in pairs.

4. Ask students to fill in the **Virtual Field Trip Log** during their visit.

EXTENSIONS AND ADAPTATIONS:

• If you are scheduled to visit the actual museum or any other location, have students conduct a virtual field trip before they go on their actual field trip. The additional knowledge should create more excitement for their trip, and students will be better prepared because they have already learned something about the destination.

• Discuss the difference between a virtual field trip and a real field trip.

• Have younger students draw a picture of their favorite exhibit on their virtual field trip rather than completing the **Virtual Field Trip Log.**

ADDITIONAL RESOURCES:

Wilson Bentley Digital Archives (Volume 1) CD-ROM—This CD can be purchased on the museum Web site. It contains over 1,000 images, articles published by and about William Bentley, as well as a complete virtual tour of the museum in Jericho, Vermont.

Snowflake Bentley Web site: **http://snowflakebentley.com/**. This site contains biographical information.

Virtual Field Trip Log

Name: _____

Date: _____

Where did you go on your field trip?

What is the URL?
http://

What was the most interesting thing that you saw?

What did you learn?

If you could take a souvenir home from your trip,
what would it be?

Figure 8.10 Virtual Field Trip Log Reproducible

Other Ideas:

- Have students conduct authentic research about William Bentley. Refer to the activity in Chapter 5, "Using the Internet for Authentic Research."

- Create your own snowflakes in a drawing program. The following Web sites provide directions for *AppleWorks* or *Microsoft Word*.

  Directions for drawing a snowflake in *Microsoft Word* or *Microsoft Powerpoint*: **http://www.microsoft.com/Education/?ID = DrawSnowflake**

  AppleWorks Educator-Specific Templates: **http://henson.austin.apple.com/ali_ appleworks/templates.htm**

- Visit the author's Web site to learn more about *Snowflake Bentley* and her other books.

  Jacqueline Briggs Martin's Home Page: **http://www.jacquelinebriggsmartin .com/**

- Have students create a timeline of William Bentley's life using the program *TimeLiner* by Tom Snyder Productions.

- Create an *Inspiration* diagram about differences and similarities in snowflakes or attributes that all snowflakes have.

- Create an *Inspiration* diagram that details the process that William Bentley went through to capture a snowflake on film.

Software Walk-throughs

Purpose of Walk-throughs

Each of the walk-throughs is designed to teach the skills addressed in the activities in this book. Each can be used by you or by your students. Each walk-through is designed so that the user can complete a project. If you are looking to advance your skills or you need more assistance with a program, try the Help menu within the program or refer to the Additional Readings that follow the References section.

Kid Pix

GOAL:

To create a simple three-picture slideshow.

BEFORE BEGINNING:

Choose a topic for a slideshow and plan what will go on each of the three pictures. In this case, the topic is "All About Me."

LET'S BEGIN:

When you open *Kid Pix Studio Deluxe,* you will be presented with six choices. In this activity, we will be using the *Kid Pix* and *Slideshow* sections of the software.

1. Click on the *Kid Pix* section on the screen. A blank piece of paper will appear. The tools appear on the left-hand side of the screen, and the Color Palette is at the bottom.

2. Type "**All About Me**" on the screen using the typewriter tool. You can enlarge the size of the font or change the appearance using the tools at the bottom of the screen. Just use the Up and Down arrows to watch the appearance change. Now type your name below the title.

3. Paint some pictures with the painting tools. You can also use the **Stamp** tool to stamp small pictures on the screen (see Figure A.1).

4. Save the picture by going to the **File** menu and dragging down to **Save.**

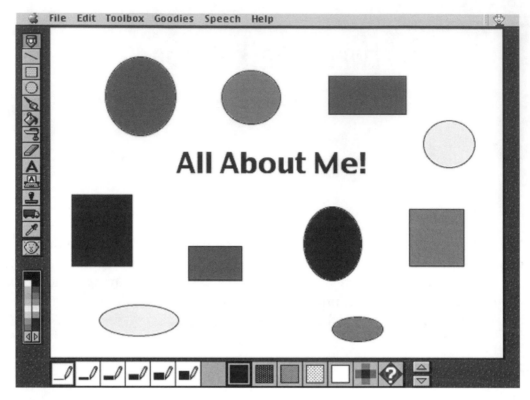

Figure A.1 Title slide

Taken from Kid Pix® Studio. ©Broderbund Properties LLC. Used with permission.

5. Type "**Title Slide**."

6. Click on the **Save** button.

7. To get a new picture go to the **File** menu and drag down to **New.** You should have a new piece of blank paper.

8. Create the next picture using a variety of tools. Draw a picture of something you like to do, and with the typewriter tool, type a sentence explaining the picture. When the picture is completed save it as "slide 2" and get another new picture.

9. Repeat the process one more time for the third picture. On this picture, draw another picture of something you like and type a sentence to go with the picture. Save this file as "slide 3."

Creating a slideshow:

1. When your final picture for the slideshow is completed and saved, go to the **File** menu and drag down to **Return to Picker.**

2. Click on the **Slideshow** option in the picker. You will see a screen with twelve small trucks (see Figure A.2). Each truck represents one slide. At the bottom of each truck are three buttons. The first button allows you to import a picture onto the truck. The second button allows you to add a sound or record your own sound,

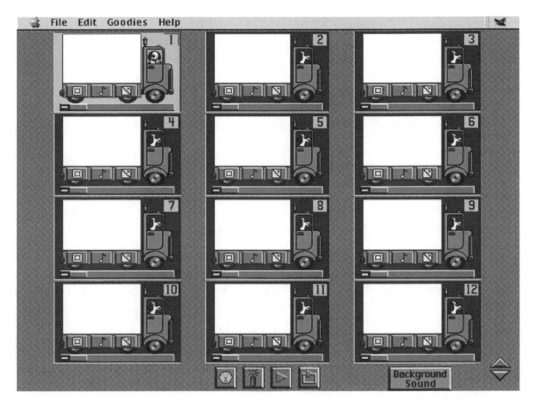

Figure A.2 Slideshow screen
Taken from Kid Pix® Studio. ©Broderbund Properties LLC. Used with permission.

and the third button allows you to choose a transition. (A transition is a special effect when one slide changes to the next.) Right below the buttons you can determine how long you wish the slide to appear on the screen when played. Drag the marker to the right to increase the time the slide is shown.

3. Start by placing your title slide on the first truck. Press the first small button, and a window will appear allowing you to select the file you saved. You may need to find the folder you originally saved the file in if your work does not appear in the window. When you find the file, click on **Open,** and a small version of your title picture should appear inside the truck.

4. Add a sound and/or transition to your slide with the other two buttons and determine how long you would like the slide to appear using the marker below.

5. Repeat this process on trucks two and three by locating your other saved files (slide 2 and slide 3). Add sounds and transitions.

6. To play your finished slideshow, use the four buttons at the bottom of the screen. The first button is for mistakes. If you added a sound or picture and you want to remove it immediately after, click on the **Face** button. The second button is for "bombing" pictures that need to be deleted from your slideshow. The third button is for playing your slideshow, and the fourth button is for playing your slideshow in a continuous loop. The **Background Sound** button to the far right allows you to

select background sounds or music to be played throughout the slideshow. Don't select this if you already chose sounds in the previous steps. Click on the third button, and your slideshow will play!

7. Don't forget to save your slideshow before quitting.

To import a graphic from another program or folder:

If you have another piece of clip-art or digital picture that you would like to use in your picture, go to the **File** menu and drag down to **Import a Graphic....** A window will appear allowing you to choose the file. Locate the file and click on **Open.** The picture should appear on the *Kid Pix* screen. Click and drag the picture to the desired location. Click once outside the picture to place it permanently.

Inspiration

GOAL:

To create a simple diagram using a variety of tools.

BEFORE BEGINNING:

Select a word or idea for a class brainstorm.

LET'S BEGIN:

Creating and linking ideas:

When you open *Inspiration* you will notice an oval in the center of the screen with the text "Main Idea." Change the main idea to **book** by replacing the words "**main idea**" with "**book**."

Now we will begin to brainstorm all the things we think of when we hear the word "book."

There are two ways to create and link other ideas to the main idea. To create ideas, click in a spot on the screen and begin typing a related idea. An oval bubble will appear as you begin typing. When the brainstorming is completed and you have several ideas around the main idea, you can link the ideas to the main idea.

To link ideas, click in the main idea. Four small squares and two small diamonds will appear around the outside of the shape. Click in a diamond and drag to the idea you want to connect to. An arrow should appear.

The alternative way to create ideas is to conduct a **RapidFire.** To do this, click in the main idea and click once behind the last letter of the word "book." You should see your blinking cursor. Now click on the **RapidFire** tool at the top of the screen. A very small lightning bolt will appear in the main idea after the word. Begin typing words that are related. After each word, hit the Return or Enter key. The words should appear outside of the main idea and should be linked to the main idea with an arrow.

You can also use the **Link** button in the toolbar at the top of the screen to link ideas to each other. The **Create** button also allows you to create new bubbles.

Changing the appearance of your ideas:

Now let's change the main idea to a picture of a book. The **Symbol Palette** should be in the left-hand corner of your screen. First, click on the main idea once to select it. (A symbol cannot be changed unless it is first selected.)

Now click on the graphic of the book, and your main idea should change to the graphic. (If your **Symbol Palette** is not on your screen, go to the **View** menu and drag down to **Symbol Palette.**)

Now let's change the ideas that link off the main idea. To select all the ideas except for the main idea, hold your **Shift** key down and click on each one you wish to change. Now that they are selected, go to the toolbar at the bottom of the page and change the fill color to white and the line color to black. Now go to the **Symbol Palette** and change the shape to the rectangle with the rounded corners. Click once outside of the ideas to deselect the group.

To resize an idea, click once on the idea and you will notice the small red squares in each corner. Click and drag on any of the squares to shrink or enlarge the shape.

To change the font or size of the words within the idea, highlight the text and go to the **Format** menu and drag down to **Font, Size,** or **Style**.

Adding a note:

Let's add a note to the main idea. What is your definition of "book"? Click once on the main idea to select it and click on the **Add Note** tool at the top of the screen. A small window should appear where you can type additional information. Type a definition for the word "book." To go back to your diagram, close the **Note** window.

Converting the diagram to outline format:

Let's convert the diagram to an outline format. This allows us to view the information in a more organized fashion. To view the diagram in outline format, click on the **Outline** tool at the top of the screen. Notes can be viewed and added in the outline view.

Arranging the diagram:

If you wish to arrange your diagram, click on the **Arrange** button in the toolbar at the top of the screen. A screen will appear presenting you with a variety of choices.

When completed, your finished diagram may resemble Figure A.3.

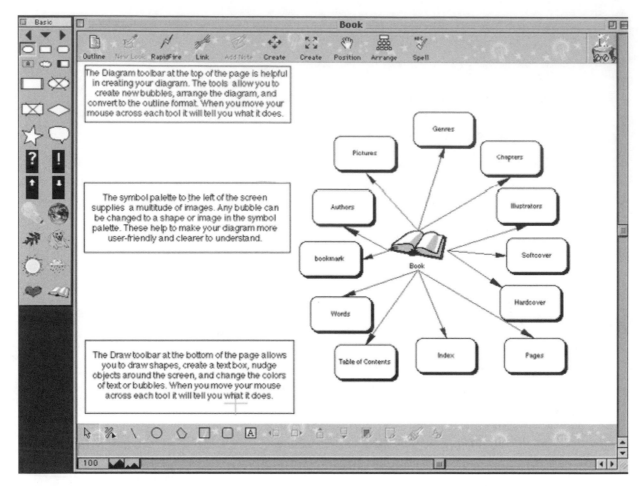

Figure A.3 Finished diagram

This diagram was created using Inspiration® by Inspiration Software®, Inc.

Hyperstudio

GOAL:

To create a five-card multimedia presentation on your favorite books with text, sounds, and pictures.

BEFORE BEGINNING:

List three titles of favorite books and their authors from your summer reading or from books you read last year. Next, list three books you might like to read during the coming year.

LET'S BEGIN:

1. Open *Hyperstudio*.

2. When the introduction screen appears, click on the button **New Stack.**

3. Click **Yes** when Addy the Dog appears.

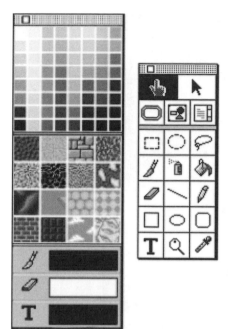

Figure A.4 Color palette and toolbar

Hyperstudio® and all of its screen images are a registered trademark of Knowledge Adventure, Inc. and are used under license.

4. Addy will appear again. Click on **Yes.**

5. Now we have our first card, and it is time to get our tools and colors ready.

Move your arrow up to the **Tools** menu. Click and hold on the word "**Tools**" and drag it to the lower left-hand corner of your screen. You should now have the toolbar on your screen. Do the same with the **Colors** menu (see Figure A.4).

THE PRESENTATION:

Card one

Your first card will be your title card. Add a title by double-clicking on the **T** tool. A screen will appear where you can select font, size, color, and style. Let's try size 48. Choose any font and color that you like! (See Figure A.5.) Click on **OK** when you have completed your choices. Click on the left-hand side of the card where you want to start the text and type "**My Favorite Books.**"

Card two

To create the next card, go to the **Edit** menu and drag down to **New Card.** Add text as you did on the title card. This time choose any font, size, style, and color you wish, but make sure the size is large enough to read. Type the title of one of your favorite books and the author name. Draw a picture of a character or scene in the book.

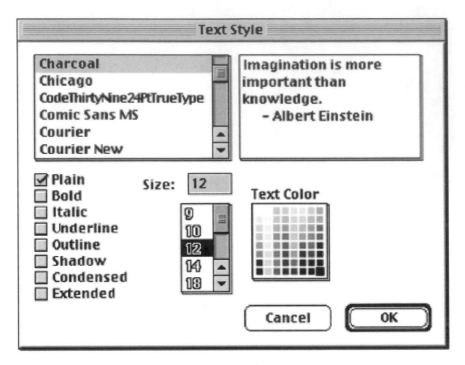

Figure A.5 Text Style window

Hyperstudio® and all of its screen images are a registered trademark of Knowledge Adventure, Inc. and are used under license.

Card three

Create a **new card.** Using the same font, size, color, and style on card two, type another favorite book title and author name. Draw a picture of a character or scene in the book.

Card four

Create a **new card.** Using the same font, size, color, and style on cards two and three, type the last favorite book title and author. Draw a picture of a character or scene in the book.

Card five—Adding a button with a sound

Create a **new card.** Using the same font, size, color, and style on cards 2, 3, and 4, type: "**Books I would like to read.**" Below the title, type the three books you want to read this year. On this card we will add a button that makes a sound. Go to the **Objects** menu and drag down to **Add a Button …** . A window will appear with choices for creating a button (see Figure A.6).

1. Where it says **Name,** type "**About Me.**"

2. On the left-hand side of the window where it says **Type,** click on the first choice.

3. On the right-hand side of the window where it says **Color,** choose a background color and a text color.

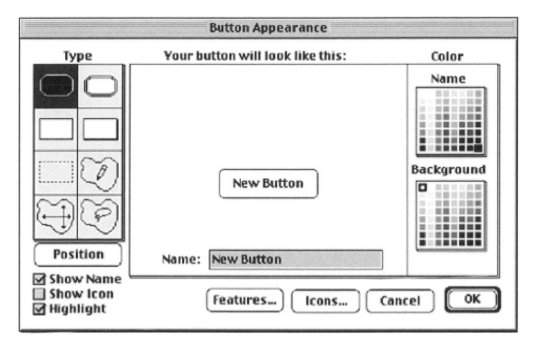

Figure A.6 Button Appearance window
*Hyperstudio® and all of its screen images are a registered trademark of Knowledge Adventure, Inc.
and are used under license.*

4. Click on **OK**.

5. You are back at the card and you need to decide where you would like the button to be placed. Click in the center of the button and drag it to the lower-half of your card.

6. Let go of the mouse and click outside of the shimmering red line.

7. The **Action** window appears for you to determine where you would like the button to go and what you would like it to do. This button will only make a sound, so click on the **Play a sound ...** box (see Figure A.7).

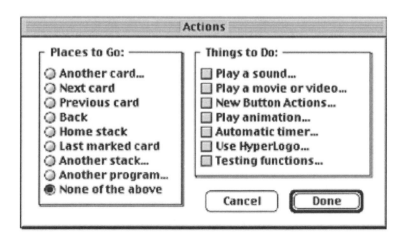

Figure A.7 Actions window
*Hyperstudio® and all of its screen images are a registered trade-
mark of Knowledge Adventure, Inc. and are used under license.*

8.   A tape deck appears. Click on the **Record** button and record yourself talking about what kind of books you like to read and what kind of a reader you are (i.e., fast reader, take your time, prefer fantasy, prefer a specific author). When you are done recording your sound, click on the **Stop** button. Click on the **Play** button to hear your recording. Click on the **OK** button to finish.

9.   You should be back in the **Action** window. Click on **Done** to finish the button.

10.   You are now back at card five. Click on the new button to hear your sound.

Adding buttons that go places!

The last thing we need to do on each card is create buttons to move through the presentation.

1.   Using the **Move** menu, drag down to the **first card** in your stack. You should be at your title card. Go to the **Objects** menu and drag down to **Add a Button ...** . A window will appear with choices for creating your button.

2.   Type the name, "**Next Card**" and choose the appearance of your button by changing the type and color. Click on **OK** and move your button to the lower right-hand corner of your card. Click outside of the red shimmering lines, and the Actions window will appear.

3.   Where it says **Places to go,** click next to **Next card.**

4.   Next you need to choose a transition. Experiment with different transitions by clicking on the button **Try it.** When you find one you like, click on **OK.**

5.   You should be back in the Actions window. Click on **Done** to finish and try out the new button.

6.   Follow this same procedure on cards two, three, and four.

Adding clip-art (Try this on card five)

1.   To add clip-art to your presentation, go to the **File** menu and pull down to **Add Clip-Art.**

2.   You should see a dialog box with a list of choices for clip-art. Click on the first one, **Addy** and click on **Open** (scc Figure A.8).

3.   Using the **Lasso** tool, draw a loop around the **Addy** that you like. Now **Addy** should have a **shimmering red line** around her.

4.   Click on **OK,** and **Addy** will be on the card.

5.   By clicking and dragging in the center of the clip-art, you can move it wherever you would like.

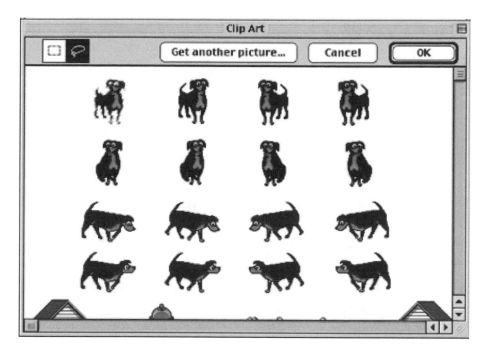

Figure A.8 Clip Art window

Hyperstudio® and all of its screen images are a registered trademark of Knowledge Adventure, Inc. and are used under license.

Cleaning up your presentation

1. To make your presentation a professional one, go to the **Edit** menu and pull down to **Preferences.**

2. Double-click on **Presentation Mode ... ,** and you should see a new window (see Figure A.9).

3. Choose a **Background Color** and uncheck **Show the Title Bar.** Click on **OK** and then click on **OK** once more. You should now see the changes.

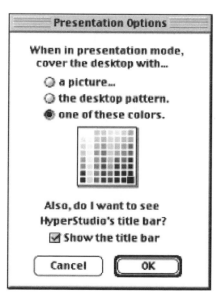

Figure A.9 Presentation Options window

Hyperstudio® and all of its screen images are a registered trademark of Knowledge Adventure, Inc. and are used under license.

OTHER USEFUL SKILLS:

Adding a text object:

A text object is useful because if you make a mistake while typing, you can go back and fix it. When you use the **T** tool and you make a mistake you have to erase the words and retype them.

1. To add a text object to your presentation, go to the **Objects** menu and pull down to **Add a Text Object.**

2. You should see an outline of a square on the card. You can move the square to a new location by clicking in the middle of the square and dragging it where you would like. You can also enlarge or shrink the square by dragging one of the corners in or out.

3. When you have the square where you would like it, click outside of the red shimmering outline. A window will appear with choices for customizing the text object (see Figure A.10).

4. Choose a text color and background color and then click on **OK.**

5. The text object will appear on the card, and you can now type text into it.

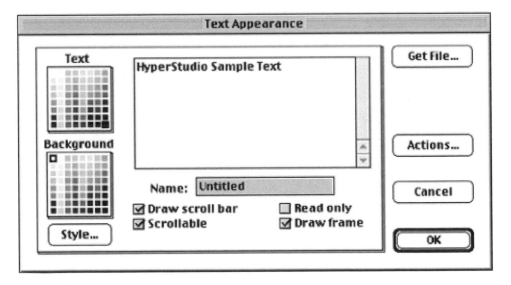

Figure A.10 Text Appearance window
Hyperstudio® and all of its screen images are a registered trademark of Knowledge Adventure, Inc. and are used under license.

AppleWorks Database

GOAL:

Creating a Simple Book Database

BEFORE BEGINNING:

Decide what fields you will include in your database and have some books available to input your first records.

LET'S BEGIN:

1. Open *AppleWorks* and select **Database** from the starting point choices.

2. A screen will appear allowing you to define the fields that will be in your database (see Figure A.11). Fields are the categories that you wish to have. It may be helpful to plan your fields out before you get onto the computer because the way in which you define them will determine how well the database can be searched or sorted later on.

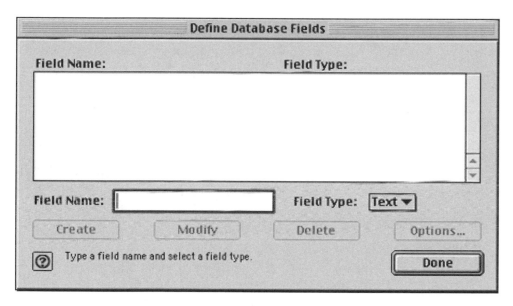

Figure A.11 Window for defining fields

3. Begin typing the names of the fields you wish to have. After each field name hit the **Enter** key or click on the **Create** button.

    Fields can be further defined by choosing whether the field will consist of words, numbers, or other items. To further define a field, click on the drop-down menu next to the words "Field Type:" and drag down to the type of field you would like to select (see Figure A.12).

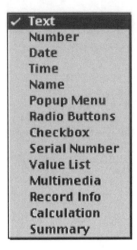

Figure A.12 Field Type pull-down menu

If it is a field where words will be typed keep it as "Text." If a number will be entered, choose "Number." "Multimedia" is great for adding pictures to a record in a database.

Try the following fields or use the fields from one of the database activities in the book:

Title

Author

Genre (Change this field type to a Pop-up menu. There will be an additional dialog box that requires you to type in the genres you want students to choose from.)

Rating (5–1) (Change this field type to a number)

Comments:

4. When all the fields are entered, click on the **Done** button. You will now see the first empty record in your database (see Figure A.13).

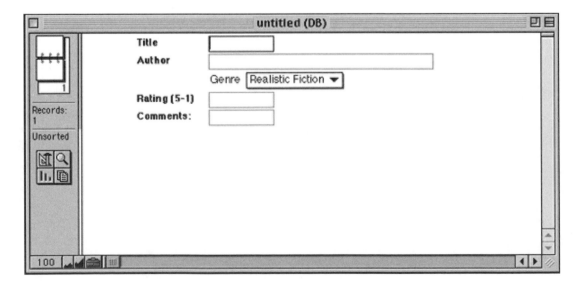

Figure A.13 View in Browse mode of an empty record

5. Now it is time to change the layout for your database. Creating or changing a layout is about designing the record to be more user friendly. It is not necessary, but it does help to make the database look nicer. Go to the **Layout** menu and drag down to **Layout.** This is the design mode of the database program (see Figure A.14). The Browse mode is for entering information into the records.

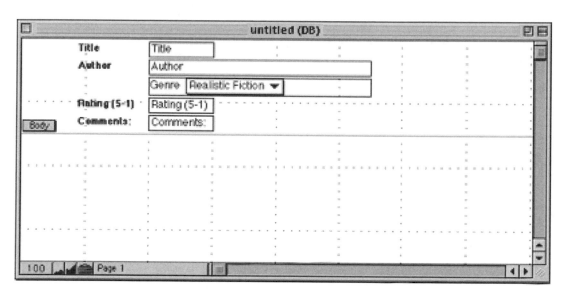

Figure A.14 View in Layout mode

6. Drag down on the box that says **Body** to create a larger space for the record.

7. Move each field where you would like it to be by clicking on the words or boxes and dragging them to new locations.

8. Make the comments and title boxes bigger to accommodate the information that will be typed. Click in a corner of the box and drag out until it reaches the size you wish.

9. Enlarge and change the fonts by clicking on a field name or box and going to the **Format** menu and pulling down to **Font, Size,** or **Style.**

10. To add a colorful background or border, use the square or oval tool to draw a shape around the field names and boxes. The shape will cover all your work, but don't panic. Next go to the **Arrange** menu and drag down to **Move to Back.** The shape should appear behind your fields. If you want the background to be colored, choose a color from the accent window.

11. If you would like the boxes to have a border around them, go to the Accent window and choose a line width from the line tab (see Figure A.15).

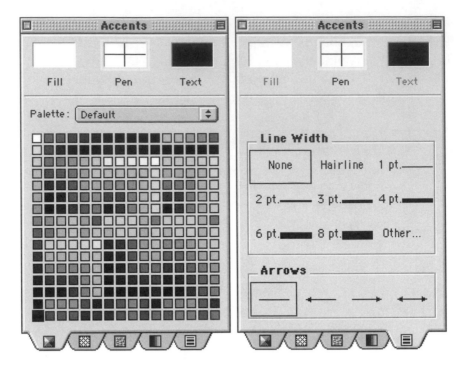

Figure A.15 Color and line choices in Accent window

12. Last, add clip-art to the layout. Go to the **File** menu and drag down to **Show Clippings** to choose from the *AppleWorks* library of clip-art. If you have other clip-art that you would like to use, go to the **File** menu and drag down to **Insert.**

13. To return to browse mode, go to the **Layout** menu and drag down to **Browse.** Now your database is ready for student input (see Figure A.16).

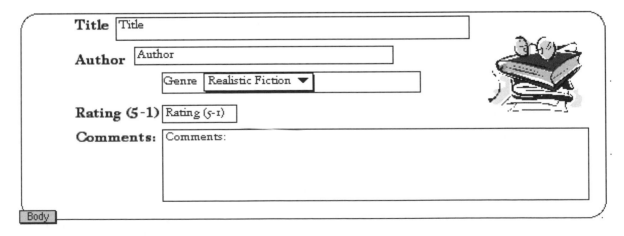

Figure A.16 Completed layout

14. To create a new record, go to the **Edit** menu and drag down to **New Record.** Don't forget to save whenever you quit!

15. To sort, go to the **Organize** menu and drag down to **Sort Records.** Move an item from the "Field List" to the "Sort Order" side to choose how to sort. You can also click on ascending or descending order.

16. To perform a find, go to the **Layout** menu and drag down to **Find.** Enter the word or item you are searching for in one particular field. Hit the **Enter** button, and any records that apply to the criteria will be located. If you want to perform another find, be sure to go to the **Organize** menu and drag down to **Show All Records.** Otherwise, the second find would only search through the records found in the previous find. To create a new layout, go to the **Layout** menu and drag down to **New Layout.** Create a layout as you did in steps 5–13.

AppleWorks Spreadsheet

GOAL:

To create a book log and learn how to input information into a spreadsheet.

BEFORE BEGINNING:

Collect any data you will need to input into the spreadsheet.

LET'S BEGIN:

(These directions will be very similar for *Microsoft Excel.*)

1. Open *AppleWorks* and select **Spreadsheet** from the starting point choices.

2. A spreadsheet will appear on the screen. A spreadsheet is made up of cells, rows, and columns. A cell is the space that you can type text, numbers, or formulas. Rows and columns are made up of several cells. A specific cell may be identified as A1 because the rows are labeled with the letters of the alphabet and the columns are labeled with numbers (see Figure A.17).

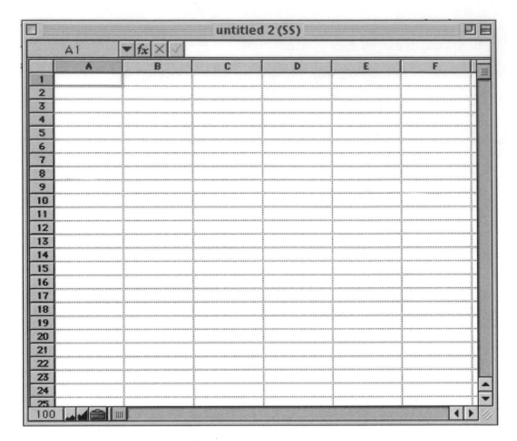

Figure A.17 Empty spreadsheet

Begin by clicking in cell A1. This is the top right cell on the spreadsheet. Now type **Date.** Hit the **Enter** key, and the word **Date** should appear in the cell.

Type "**Title and Author**" in B1

Type "**Pages Read**" in C1

3. Now we are going to stretch out the column width. To change the size of the first column, click on cell A1 and go to the **Format** menu and pull down to **Column width....** In the box, change the number to **100** and click on **OK.** Now change the second column to **375** and the third column to **165.**

4. Fill in the **Date** column with the dates from one month of school. In the example, the dates were from the month of May. Fill in the **Title and Author** column with the book you were reading on each day of the month. Fill in the **Pages Read** column with how many pages were read each day. (Students can log this in a reading journal and later input the information into the spreadsheet.)

5. In cell B33, enter the text, "**Average Number of Pages Read.**"

   In cell B34, enter the text, "**Total Pages Read in May.**" (Or whatever month you chose.)

   In cell B35, enter the text, "**Number of Books Finished.**"

6. Now we are ready to learn how to make formulas. Formulas make our job easier by doing the math like a calculator. Click in cell C33. This is where the **Average Number of Pages Read** number will appear. Type the following formula: = **Average (C2..C32)**

   This formula means that the average of cell C2 through C32 will appear in this cell. You can also type = **Average** (and then drag through C2 to C32 and then close the formula with a parentheses).

   In cell C34, type the following formula: "= **SUM(C2..C32)**" This formula means that the sum of cell C2 through C32 will appear in this cell.

7. In cell C35, type the number of books that were completed in the month. No formula can be used for this cell.

8. Highlight the last three rows of information including the end of the month statistics and make them bold by going to the **Format** menu and dragging down to **Style** and then over to **Bold.**

9. If you wish, add clip-art to the spreadsheet to represent each book. Go to the **File** menu and drag down to **Insert** to find clip-art on your computer or drag down to **Show Clippings** to choose from the *AppleWorks* library of clip-art. In the example there are student drawings that were copied and pasted from another drawing program (see Figure A.18).

	A	B	C
1	Date	Title and Author	Pages Read
2	5/1/02	Amber Brown is not a Crayon by Paula Danziger	6
3	5/2/02	Amber Brown is not a Crayon by Paula Danziger	7
4	5/3/02	Amber Brown is not a Crayon by Paula Danziger	10
5	5/4/02	Amber Brown is not a Crayon by Paula Danziger	0
6	5/5/02	Amber Brown is not a Crayon by Paula Danziger	9
7	5/6/02	Amber Brown is not a Crayon by Paula Danziger	9
8	5/7/02	Amber Brown is not a Crayon by Paula Danziger	10
9	5/8/02	Amber Brown is not a Crayon by Paula Danziger	12
10	5/9/02	Amber Brown is not a Crayon by Paula Danziger	12
11	5/10/02	The Littles by John Peterson	10
12	5/11/02	The Littles by John Peterson	7
13	5/12/02	The Littles by John Peterson	8
14	5/13/02	The Littles by John Peterson	5
15	5/14/02	The Littles by John Peterson	9
16	5/15/02	The Littles by John Peterson	6
17	5/16/02	The Littles by John Peterson	10
18	5/17/02	The Littles by John Peterson	9
19	5/18/02	The Littles by John Peterson	8
20	5/19/02	The Littles by John Peterson	0
21	5/20/02	The Littles by John Peterson	8
22	5/21/02	Ramona the Pest by Beverly Cleary	7
23	5/22/02	Ramona the Pest by Beverly Cleary	9
24	5/23/02	Ramona the Pest by Beverly Cleary	9
25	5/24/02	Ramona the Pest by Beverly Cleary	8
26	5/25/02	Ramona the Pest by Beverly Cleary	0
27	5/26/02	Ramona the Pest by Beverly Cleary	10
28	5/27/02	Ramona the Pest by Beverly Cleary	7
29	5/28/02	Ramona the Pest by Beverly Cleary	9
30	5/29/02	Ramona the Pest by Beverly Cleary	6
31	5/30/02	Ramona the Pest by Beverly Cleary	9
32	5/31/02	Ramona the Pest by Beverly Cleary	8
33		Average Number of Pages Read	7.6451612903
34		Total Pages read in May	237
35		Number of Books Finished	2

Figure A.18 Completed spreadsheet

TO MAKE A GRAPH:

1. Click in Cell C1 and drag down through cell C33. Do not include cells C34 or C35.

2. Go to the **Options** menu and drag down to **Make a Chart ...** .

3. Next choose the type of graph to display the **Number of Pages Read** each day. In this example, a line graph might be useful in looking at the student's reading patterns. Explore the other options on the left-hand side of the chart choices to alter the graph in other ways (see Figure A.19).

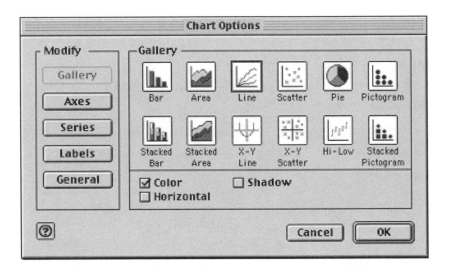

Figure A.19 Chart Options window

4. Click on **OK.** A graph will appear on the spreadsheet (see Figure A.20).

5. Optional: If you would like the graph to be in a separate file, go to the **Edit** menu and **Copy** the graph. Create a new word processing or drawing file and go to the **Edit** menu and **Paste** the graph.

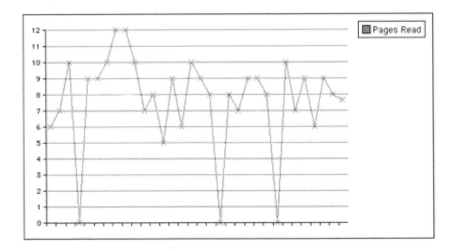

Figure A.20 Line graph

Saving Templates

Saving a file as a template makes it impossible for your students to erase the original file you worked so hard to create. When they open a template, the file becomes a new untitled file that requires them to save it with a new name when they are done. If students make a mistake, alter or delete a part of the template that is necessary, they can simply close the file and reopen the template you created. Templates are useful when you want to give guidelines for a technology project. For example, in a newsletter you would want students to type their text in specific columns and add their graphics to other places. Some templates are packaged with the software program so you do not have to spend the time to create them.

To save your own templates follow these directions:

In *AppleWorks*:

1. Go to the **File** menu and drag down to **Save As.**

2. In the **Save** box, click on the button next to the word "Template." This appears in the lower right-hand corner (see Figure A.21).

3. Locate the folder in which you would like to save your template.

4. Name your template and hit the **Save** button.

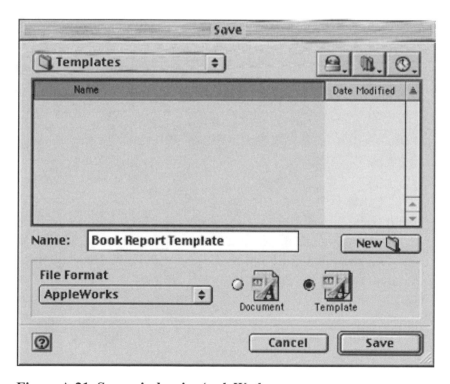

Figure A.21 Save window in *AppleWorks*

In *Microsoft Word*:

1. Go to the **File** menu and drag down to **Save As.**

2. In the **Save** box, click on the drop-down menu labeled **Format.** This appears below the name of the file. Select **Document Template** (see Figure A.22).

3. Locate the folder in which you would like to save your template.

4. Name your template and hit the **Save** button.

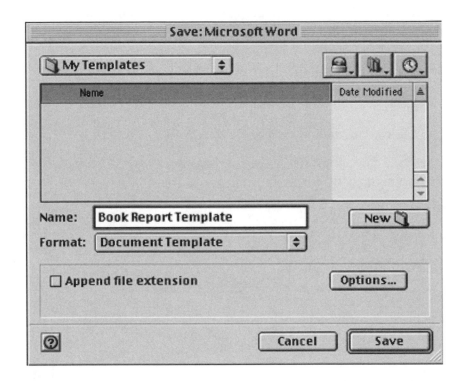

Figure A.22 Save window in *Microsoft Word*

Copy, Cut, and Paste

Copy and paste is a skill we need to learn for ourselves and to teach our students. It allows us to get our work done faster and easier. Copying and pasting allows us to take a group of text or graphics and move them to a new location without retyping or creating them again. If you copy text, it stays where it was originally and then you can paste it into a new location. If you cut text, it removes it from the original location and allows you to paste it to a new location. The how-to of copying and pasting is very similar on both PCs and Macintosh systems.

To copy and paste text:

1. Locate the text you would like to copy and drag over it to highlight the words. Begin with the first word or letter and drag to the last.

2. Go to the **Edit** menu and drag down to **Copy.**

3. Create a new file or find the location where you would like to place the copied text.

4. Go to the **Edit** menu again and drag down to **Paste.** The text should appear!

TO COPY GRAPHICS:

1. Locate the graphic you would like to copy and click on it once to select it.

2. Go to the **Edit** menu and drag down to **Copy.**

3. Create a new file or find the location where you would like to place the copied graphic.

4. Go to the **Edit** menu again and drag down to **Paste.** The graphic should appear!

   To cut text or graphics, alter step 2 by going to the **Edit** menu and dragging down to **Cut.**

GRABBING AN IMAGE FROM THE INTERNET:

Macintosh directions:

1. Click and hold your mouse on the image, and a menu should pop up to the right.

2. Drag down to **Download Image to Disk.**

3. You will see a **Save** box appear. Find the location on your computer where you would like to save and click on the **Save** button.

PC directions:

1. Right-click on the image you want to download, and a menu should pop up to the right.

2. Drag down to **Download Image to Disk.**

3. You will see a **Save** box appear. Find the location on your computer where you would like to save and click on the **Save** button.

Planning Sheets, Rubrics, and Checklists

Planning sheets allow students to think through their project before working on the computer. Students can become overwhelmed with the tools available to them. If they plan their projects carefully, though, the computer time should be more productive. With planning sheets, you can also check on students' progress as they are working and redirect them if they are off-task. Along with the planning sheets you will find a few assessment tools for multimedia projects. The assessment tools are meant for teacher, peer, and individual evaluation. They should assist students in creating better projects. Make sure students have the assessment tools available before they begin so they can continually check on their own progress. If you would like to use the rubric or checklist to give a grade, assign point values to each category. The checklist requirements have been left open so that you can decide what is required for a specific project. Several Web sites have rubrics and other assessment tools available. If you want to create your own rubric online, try the RubiStar Web site: **http://rubistar.4teachers.org.**

Multimedia Planning Sheet

Name:

Notes:

_____

_____

_____

_____

_____

_____

_____

_____

_____

_____

_____

Figure B.1 Multimedia Planning Sheet

Kid Pix Planning Sheet

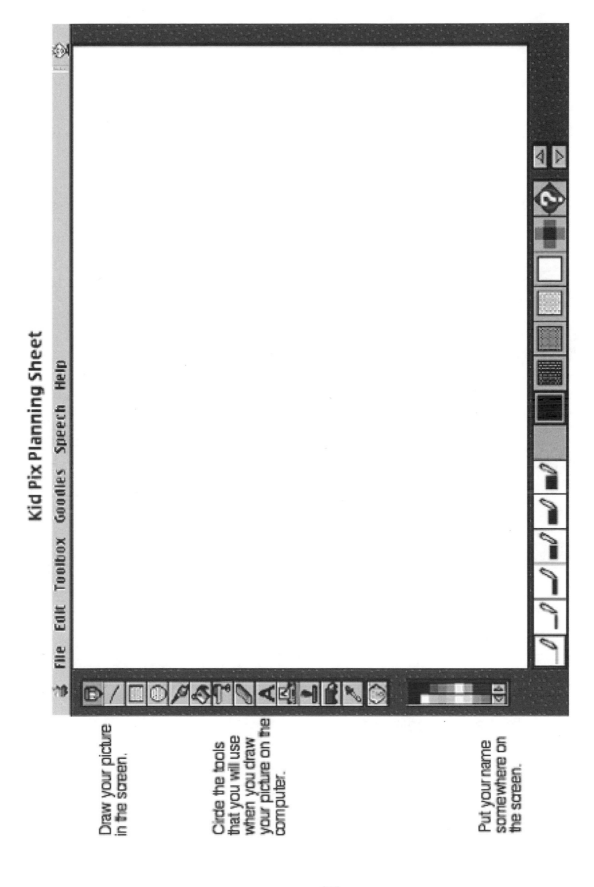

File   Edit   Toolbox   Goodies   Speech   Help

Draw your picture in the screen.

Circle the tools that you will use when you draw your picture on the computer.

Put your name somewhere on the screen.

Figure B.2 *Kid Pix* Planning Sheet

217

Multimedia Rubric

Name:_____

Information

Did you include the information you needed to?
Will someone else learn something new?
Did you use your own words?
Is it interesting?

1   2   3   4   5

How does it look?

Do you have a title card?
Did you draw or choose clip-art that goes with your topic?
Is it interesting to look at?

1   2   3   4   5

Mechanics

Did you check your spelling and punctuation?

1   2   3   4   5

Technical

Did you learn how to do something new?
If there are buttons, do they work and go to the correct cards?
Did you use any sound?
Did you use any clip-art?
Did you add an animations?

1   2   3   4   5

What was your final score?_____

Figure B.3 Multimedia Rubric

Multimedia Checklist

Name:_____

Requirements:

_____

_____

_____

_____

_____

_____

Extras that I tried:

_____

_____

_____

_____

Check the statement that best applies to your work:

Check the statement that best applies to your work:

_____My presentation was better technically. (Good design, buttons work, etc.)

_____My presentation was stronger in content. (Necessary facts, teaches someone something new.)

_____My presentation was well-balanced.

Figure B.4 Multimedia Checklist

Children's Literature Web Sites

Between the Lions

http://pbskids.org/lions/index.html

You can find a new story on this PBS Web site each week along with related activities.

Book Adventure

http://www.bookadventure.com/

Try out this reading incentive program with your students. Students read a book, take a quiz, and can earn points toward prizes. Book Adventure was created by the Sylvan Learning Foundation and is a nonprofit organization. There are sections for parents, teachers, and kids. This is a great site to recommend for parents for the summer months.

BookHive

http://www.bookhive.org/

Here is another Web site with many reviews of books. Students can also add their own favorite booklist to the Web site.

Carol Hurst's Children's Literature Site

http://www.carolhurst.com/

This site has a collection of book reviews, ways to use literature in the classroom, activities, and information on the most current teaching strategies with children's literature.

Doucette Index: K-12 Literature-Based Teaching Ideas: An Index to Books and Websites

http://www.educ.ucalgary.ca/litindex/

Use the search engine on this site to search for books and Web sites that have activities and ideas for teaching with specific book titles.

Mightybook.com

http://www.mightybook.com/

This site has read-aloud stories that students can read along with or listen to. There are many other fun activities for students to discover.

Mona Kerby's The Reading Corner

http://ccpl.carr.lib.md.us/read/

This site is composed of book reviews for young readers. This is a great resource for selecting a book to read. Students or teachers can narrow their search by genre.

New York Public Library: On-Lion for Kids!

http://www2.nypl.org/home/branch/kids/

Visit the New York Public Library online and browse through their information on children's books and authors. There is also a collection of Internet links for teachers, students, or parents.

Reading Rainbow: Kids

http://gpn.unl.edu/rainbow/

The official site for Reading Rainbow has activities centering around the many books discussed on the show. There are also contests and ideas for teachers and parents.

StoryBook Online

http://www.storybookonline.net/main.html

Another great site for finding stories online.

The Children's Literature Web Guide

http://www.ucalgary.ca/~dkbrown/index.html

This is a collection of some of the best Web sites regarding children's literature.

World of Reading

http://www.worldreading.org/

Find links to many authors and have students submit their own book reviews using this site.

References

Children's Literature

Aardema, Verna. *Why Mosquitoes Buzz in People's Ears.* New York: The Dial Press, 1975.

Adler, David A. *Cam Jansen and the Mystery of the Gold Coins.* Illustrated by Susanna Natti. New York: Viking Penguin, 1982.

Ahlberg, Janet and Allan. *The Jolly Postman or Other People's Letters.* Boston: Little, Brown and Company, 1986.

Almond, David. *Skellig.* New York: Delacorte Press, 1999.

Baron, Kathy. *The Tree of Time.* Yosemite National Park, CA: Yosemite Association, 1994.

Bentley, W. A., and W. J. Humphreys. *Snow Crystals.* New York: Dover Publications, Inc., 1962.

Brett, Jan. *Goldilocks and the Three Bears.* New York: G. P. Putnam and Sons, 1990.

Brown, Marc. *Arthur's Mystery Envelope.* New York: Little, Brown and Company, 1998.

Bunting, Eve. *Fly Away Home.* Illustrated by Ronald Himler. New York: Clarion, 1991.

Burns, Marilyn. *The Greedy Triangle.* Illustrated by Gordon Silveria. New York: Scholastic Inc., 1994.

Cannon, Janell. *Stellaluna.* New York: Harcourt Brace and Company, 1993.

Carle, Eric. *Pancakes, Pancakes!* New York: Simon and Schuster, 1990.

Cherry, Lynne. *The Armadillo from Amarillo.* San Diego: Harcourt Brace and Company, 1994.

Clements, Andrew. *Frindle.* Illustrated by Brian Selznick. New York: Simon and Schuster, 1996.

Cooney, Barbara. *Miss Rumphius.* New York: Viking Penguin, Inc., 1982.

Creech, Sharon. *Love that Dog.* New York: HarperCollins Publishers, 2001.

Crilley, Mark. *Akiko on the Planet Smoo.* New York: Random House, Inc., 2000.

Cronin, Doreen. *Click, Clack, Moo Cows that Type.* Illustrated by Betsy Lewin. New York: Simon and Schuster, 2000.

Day, Alexandra. *Good Dog Carl.* New York: Scholastic, 1985.

De Beer, Hans. *Little Polar Bear.* New York: Scholastic Inc., 1995.

El Nabli, Dina. "Bush Proposes New Government Department." *Time for Kids.com* (June 7, 2002): http://www.timeforkids.com/TFK/news/story

Estes, Eleanor. *The Hundred Dresses.* Illustrated by Louis Slobodkin. San Diego: Harcourt Brace, 1974.

Fendler, Donn. *Lost on a Mountain in Maine.* Edited by Joseph B. Egan. New York: Beech Tree Books, 1992.

Fleischman, Sid. *The Whipping Boy.* New York: William Morrow and Co., 1987.

Gantos, Jack. *Joey Pigza Swallowed the Key.* New York: Farrar, Straus and Giroux, 1998.

Gorbachev, Valeri. *Goldilocks and the Three Bears.* New York: North-South Books, 2001.

Gurney, James. *Dinotopia.* Atlanta: Turner Publishing, Inc., 1992.

Hansen, T. Cory. *The Last Little Pumpkin.* Illustrated by Carol Foldvary-Anderson. Reno, NV: JetKor, 2001.

Hazen, Barbara Shook. *Tight Times.* New York: Viking, 1979.

Howe, Deborah and James. *Bunnicula.* Illustrated by Alan Daniel. New York: Scholastic, 1979.

Jacques, Brian. *Redwall.* New York: Philomel Books, 1986.

Juster, Norton. *The Phantom Tollbooth.* New York: Random House, Inc., 1961.

Kerley, Barbara. *The Dinosaurs of Waterhouse Hawkins.* Illustrated by Brian Selznick. New York: Scholastic, Inc., 2001

Knight, Margy Burns. *Talking Walls.* Illustrated by Anne Sibley O'Brien. Gardiner, Maine: Tilbury House Publishers, 1992.

Koch, Kenneth, and Kate Farrell. *Talking to the Sun.* New York: The Metropolitan Museum of Art, 1985.

Landon, Lucinda. *Meg Mackintosh and the Mystery at Camp Creepy.* North Scituate, RI: Secret Passage Press, 1990.

Le, Marianne. *Mousie's Adventures.* The Internet Public Library (June 1, 2002): http://www.ipl.org/div/kidspace/storyhour/

Le Guin, Ursula K. *Catwings.* Illustrated by S.D. Schindler. New York: Scholastic, Inc., 1988.

Levine, Gail Carson. *Ella Enchanted.* New York: HarperCollins Publishers Inc., 1997.

Lewis, C. S. *The Lion, the Witch and the Wardrobe.* Illustrated by Pauline Baynes. New York: HarperCollins, 1994.

Lineker, Gary. *The Young Soccer Player.* New York: DK Publishing, Inc., 1994.

Lionni, Leo. *Swimmy.* New York: Pantheon Books, 1968.

Lord, Bette Bao. *In the Year of the Boar and Jackie Robinson.* Illustrated by Marc Simont. New York: Harper and Row, 1984.

Lowry, Lois. *Number the Stars.* New York: Bantam Doubleday Dell Publishing Group, Inc., 1989.

Macaulay, David. *Pyramid.* Boston: Houghton Mifflin Company, 1975.

MacLachlan, Patricia. *Sarah, Plain and Tall.* New York: HarperCollins Publishers, 1985.

Mado, Michio. *The Animals.* Translated by The Empress Michiko of Japan. Illustrated by Mitsumasa Anno. New York: Macmillan Publishing Company, 1992.

Marshall, James. *Goldilocks and the Three Bears.* New York: Dial Books for Young Readers, 1988.

Martin, Jacqueline Briggs. *Snowflake Bentley.* Illustrated by Mary Azarian. Boston: Houghton Mifflin Company, 1998.

McDonald, Megan. *The Potato Man.* New York: Orchard Books, 1991.

McLerran, Alice. *Roxaboxen.* Illustrated by Barbara Cooney. New York: Viking Penguin, 1991.

Mowatt, Farley. *Owls in the Family.* Boston: Little, Brown and Company, 1962.

Numeroff, Laura Joffe. *If You Give a Mouse a Cookie.* Illustrated by Felicia Bond. New York: Harper, 1985.

Osbourne, Mary Pope. *Mystery under the May-Apple.* New York: Random House Inc., 1992.

Perrault, Charles. *Cinderella.* Retold by Amy Ehrlich. Illustrated by Susan Jeffers. New York: Dial Books for Young Readers, 1985.

Pilkey, Dav. *Twas the Night before Thanksgiving.* New York: Scholastic, 1990.

Prelutsky, Jack. *The 20th Century Children's Poetry Treasury.* Illustrated by Meilo So. New York: Alfred A. Knopf, 1999.

———. *Something Big Has Been Here.* Illustrated by James Stevenson. New York: William Morrow and Company, Inc., 1990.

Priceman, Marjorie. *How to Make an Apple Pie and See the World.* New York: Alfred A. Knopf, 1994.

Rowling, J.K. *Harry Potter and the Sorcerer's Stone.* New York: Scholastic, Inc., 1997.

Sachar, Louis. *Holes.* New York: Random House, Inc., 1998.

Say, Allen. *Grandfather's Journey.* Boston: Houghton Mifflin Company, 1993.

Seuss, Dr. *Green Eggs and Ham.* New York: Beginner Books, 1960.

Sobel, Donald. *Encyclopedia Brown Takes the Case.* Illustrated by Leonard Shortall. New York: Elsevier-Dutton Publishing Company, Inc., 1973.

St. George, Judith. *So You Want to Be President.* Illustrated by David Small. New York: Penguin Putnam Books, 2000.

Steig, William. *Amos and Boris.* New York: Farrar, Straus and Giroux, 1971.

Swinburne, Stephen R. *Unbeatable Beaks.* Illustrated by Joan Paley. New York: Henry Holt and Company, 1999.

Van Allsburg, Chris. *The Stranger.* Boston: Houghton Mifflin, 1986.

———. *The Wreck of the Zephyr.* Boston: Houghton Mifflin, 1983.

Waber, Bernard. *Ira Sleeps Over.* Boston: Houghton Mifflin, 1972.

White, E. B. *Stuart Little.* Illustrated by Garth Williams. New York: HarperCollins, 1945.

Wilder, Laura Ingalls. *Little House on the Prairie.* New York: HarperCollins, 1953.

Zolotow, Charlotte. *The Seashore Book.* New York: HarperCollins, 1992.

Professional Selections

Daniels, Harvey. *Literature Circles: Voice and Choice in Book Clubs and Reading Groups.* York, ME: Stenhouse Publishers, 2001.

Eeds, Maryann, and Ralph Peterson. *Grand Conversations.* New York: Scholastic, Inc., 1990.

Goudvis, Anne, and Stephanie Harvey. *Strategies that Work: Teaching Comprehension to Enhance Understanding.* York, ME: Stenhouse Publishers, 2000.

Keene, Ellin Oliver, and Susan Zimmermann. *Mosaic of Thought.* Portsmouth, NH: Heinemann, 1997.

Additional Readings

Daniels, Harvey. *Literature Circles: Voice and Choice in Book Clubs and Reading Groups*. York, ME: Stenhouse Publishers, 2001

Eeds, Maryann, and Ralph Peterson. *Grand Conversations*. New York: Scholastic, Inc., 1990.

Fleck, Tim. *Hyperstudio for Terrified Teachers-Grades 3–5*. Westminster, CA: Teacher Created Materials, 1997.

Goudvis, Anne, and Stephanie Harvey. *Strategies that Work: Teaching Comprehension to Enhance Understanding*. York, ME: Stenhouse Publishers, 2000.

Keene, Ellin Oliver, and Susan Zimmermann. *Mosaic of Thought*. Portsmouth, NH: Heinemann, 1997.

Lifter, Marcia. *KidPix for Terrified Teachers-Grade K–2*. Westminster, CA: Teacher Created Materials, 1997.

Muir, Michael. *But How Do I Use Hyperstudio with Kids: Designing and Doing Curriculum-Based Projects*. Eugene, OR: International Society for Technology in Education, 1997.

Patton, Paula G. *Microsoft Word for Terrified Teachers*. Westminster, CA: Teacher Created Materials, 1999.

Rosengart, Terry. *AppleWorks for Terrified Teachers*. Westminster, CA: Teacher Created Materials, 2001.

———. *Inspiration for Terrified Teachers*. Westminster, CA: Teacher Created Materials, 2000.

Credits

Adobe Acrobat® eBook Reader™
Adobe and the Adobe logo are either registered trademarks or trademarks of Adobe Systems Incorporated in the United States and/or other countries.

Apple
Screenshots reprinted by permission from Apple Computer, Inc.

Dav Pilkey's WEBSITE O'FUN
Screenshots from AUTHOR AND ILLUSTRATOR DAV PILKEY'S WEBSITE O'FUN. Copyright ©1997 by Dav Pilkey. Reprinted by permission of Writers House, LLC.

EPALS Classroom Exchange™
©1996–2002 ePALS Classroom Exchange, Inc.™

Hyperstudio®
Hyperstudio® and all of its screen images is a registered trademark of Knowledge Adventure, Inc. and is used under license.

Inspiration®
The diagrams in this book were created using Inspiration® by Inspiration Software®, Inc.

Kid Pix® Studio
Taken from Kid Pix® Studio. ©Broderbund Properties LLC. Used with permission.

The Internet Public Library
Graphics courtesy of The Internet Public Library ©2002 The Regents of the University of Michigan.

The Last Little Pumpkin
Author T. Cory Hansen, Illustrator Carol Foldvary-Anderson
Published by JetKor, Reno, Nevada ©2001.
Phone (775)846-1185

Skellig by David Almond
Excerpt from SKELLIG by David Almond, copyright ©1998 by David Almond. Used by permission of Random House Children's Books, a division of Random House, Inc.

TimeLiner™ 5.0
Graphics from TimeLiner™ 5.0 from Tom Snyder Productions

Index